The Bowel Book
A Practical Guide to Good Health

by David Ehrlich
with George Wolf

Foreword by Peter Albright, M.D.

Schocken Books • New York

First published by Schocken Books 1981
10 9 8 7 6 5 4 3   83 84

Copyright © 1981 by Schocken Books Inc.

Library of Congress Cataloging in Publication Data

Ehrlich, David, 1941–
    The bowel book.

    Includes index.

    1. Intestines.   2. Defecation.   3. Health.
I. Wolf, George, 1934–   joint author. II. Title.
QP156.E35   613   80–54140

Designed by Gloria Gentile
Manufactured in the United States of America
ISBN 0–8052–3763–1 hardback
        0–8052–0673–6 paperback

To MAX EHRLICH, M.D.,
whose life has been
dedicated to the
art of healing

CONTENTS

Foreword

PETER ALBRIGHT, M.D.

The Bowel Book is a concise and accurate guide to digestion and elimination and the problems associated with these functions. It offers highly practical and useful advice on the prevention and cure of the most common bowel complaints, including constipation, diarrhea, flatulence, and hemorrhoids. Drawing on the most advanced medical knowledge as well as data from naturopathic and homeopathic practitioners, the authors provide a clear and reasonable approach to gastrointestinal health.

Some readers may feel put off by the subject of this book and it is undeniable that there is a strong taboo about the discussion and understanding of bowel function. Whatever its origins, however, it seems clear that the persistence of this taboo only results in a kind of ignorance about our health with which we can ill afford to live. Just as Victorian attitudes toward the discussion of sex led to a great deal of misinformation on that subject for young people—and only now are we beginning to provide adequate and unembarrassed advice to young people—so the refusal to discuss bowel function has led not only to misunderstanding, but even to physical discomfort and illness. In this context, *The Bowel Book* is a pioneering effort that begins to reshape our thinking and feelings about bowel function by bringing the subject out into the open. The publication of this book should not only help us feel healthier, but allow us generally to feel better about this vital area of our experience.

David Ehrlich and George Wolf provide advice that is based on the assumption that we are complex beings, that no two of us are identical, but that all of us possess that capacity to take control of our lives and our health. It is with this understanding—which, by the way, is one of the foundations for the holistic health movement—that the authors urge the reader to be more aware of the signals the body sends out, to be aware of the warning signs of imbalance of physical function so that we can do the things that are necessary to correct them and avoid the more serious problems that may irreversibly damage our health. With common sense and sound information of the sort provided in this book we should be able to keep our gastrointestinal systems functioning in a healthy way and avoid the need for the wide array of chemical remedies that fill newspapers and television.

The Bowel Book has a serious set of purposes which are carried out very well indeed. This is done in an informal and friendly style, and with good humor, but the seriousness of the task of the book is never lost sight of—to bring the subject of digestive function and elimination out of our culture's closet into the light of day.

As each layer of misconception and misinformation in our lives is stripped away, we become more enlightened beings. *The Bowel Book* performs this service in an excellent way for us in a very important area of our experience which has been hitherto virtually unexplored in full view of the public.

Introduction

Medical science has made amazing progress in understanding the workings of the human gastrointestinal system. As a result, we are now able to prevent, control, and cure many serious and life-threatening diseases which claimed countless lives not so long ago. There is a great gap between the knowledge of scientists and the knowledge of the general public. Many facts, theories, and new treatments are totally unknown to the average American. One reason for this is that the average person assumes that he is unable to understand the ideas. But they are really quite simple when translated from medical jargon to everyday language. Some of the gap is caused by the way new medical data are disseminated. New discoveries are first directed toward the specialist—that is, the medical researcher, the practicing physician, and other members of the health community. At this level, the data are presented through lectures at conventions, through articles in professional journals, and through specialized textbooks. Here the language is highly technical. Specialized jargon is used, complicated statistical formulae are employed, and a broad and deep understanding of basic fields such as physiology, anatomy, pathology, and pharmacology are assumed. The average layman has as much chance of getting any information out of these sources as he does from reading hieroglyphics. Furthermore, the average medical researcher cannot afford the time to convey his discovery to the general public. His job is simply to make sure that it reaches the health community, and all too often this is where it stops.

Our aim in this book is to bring you the most fundamental and the most recent facts and concepts from a very important field of medicine dealing with your bowels. Thus we translate from medical jargon to simple everyday language. We have endeavored to do this without compromising accuracy, detail, or significance, or losing the excitement of discovery and learning.

You may already know something about a few of the things we are going to tell you in this book. You are undoubtedly concerned about every aspect of your health—nutrition, exercise, emotional relaxation, and of course, proper elimination. Perhaps you have always wondered whether your elimination was really up to par, whether it could be improved in any way, or how much influence it has on your total well-being. There is a good chance that you were never really given much information about the area except for the oft-repeated truisms that "everyone has his own rhythm, so don't worry"; or "You'll be all right in a couple of days, so chew another chocolate laxative and get some sleep." The fact that you picked up this book shows that you were dissatisfied with these kinds of answers. We, ourselves, have been extremely dissatisfied with the popular literature on the subject and felt the compelling need to contribute our knowledge and research to an area that is so obviously of vital importance to health.

We want not only to enlighten you but to arouse in you a healthy and open attitude toward your natural processes. Your emotional state and your evaluative judgments are extremely important to healthy elimination. If you feel elimination is a "dirty" bodily function, you will tend to put it off or to get it over with as quickly as possible. And thus you do a severe injustice to your body. Do you realize that there are peoples of the world who view the elimination period as one of the most significant times of the day, as a moment most conducive to meditation and general equilibrium? How different from our typically American attitude of "quickly getting the job done."

Why is bowel hygiene important? The eliminatory process is really quite complicated and extremely sensitive. The delicate balance and regularity which are necessary for the best functioning of the body can be easily disturbed by a variety of factors—improper diet, bacterial infections, insufficient exercise, and especially psychological factors such as your moods, your tensions, your fears, and your conscious and unconscious attitudes. When these factors cause improper processing of foods, some serious problems can arise—poisoning of the blood, headaches, bloating, gas, ulceration of the intestines, hemorrhoids, arthritis, and diverticulosis. We feel that everyone can profit from this book. Few of us in this country are totally free of problems in elimination. It is almost as if we had forgotten how to move our bowels. Indeed, we may even have forgotten the reason why. We hope to aid you in improving your elimination to the point where it is one of your most healthy and invigorating bodily functions, rather than your most neglected and dangerously misused one.

The booksellers' shelves are extremely well supplied with popularized accounts of recent discoveries and theories on nutrition and even digestion, but have you ever noticed any books on the process of elimination? You can follow your doctor's recommendations to the letter. You can even get all your food at the organic food store, but if your eliminary system is not working properly, your entire body will suffer. Laxatives are sold like aspirin in drugstores and supermarkets as if constipation were as common as the cold; and yet, where can you find the simplest information about why you are constipated in the first place? The sad fact is that there is not an abundance of medical literature on eliminatory processes per se. Why is this? We must assume that the subject is not very attractive to young researchers and thus they direct their scientific work elsewhere. Furthermore, the average writer on health would rather deal with the relatively safe ground of what foods to eat to enable you to run like a Hunza or swim like a Polynesian.

The whole topic of elimination is full of emotional taboos. Just think of almost any word that we use to describe this most important process and you will find that it doubles as a "dirty word." Our early training tends to make us look at our elimination with revulsion or shame instead of with a mature acceptance of what is a natural and necessary link in the cyclical process of cleansing and building the body. In our book, we attempt to get at the roots of society's self-defeating attitudes toward our bowels, and to guide you toward a more thorough understanding and pride in all your bodily processes. We have chosen a title for our book that is direct and forthright, and despite the embarrassment that our subject may cause, we have at all times attempted to treat it openly. By this means we hope not only to communicate our material to you more effectively, but also to encourage a more open and direct discussion of bowel health throughout our society.

Our plan is to combine and synthesize three great sources of knowledge which are most relevant to the problems of elimination. The first and most obvious source is modern medical physiology. Here we obtained our information from leading authoritative textbooks of medical physiology, pathology, and proctology; and medical research journals such as the *Journal of the American Medical Association*, the *Journal of Pharmacology and Experimental Therapeutics*, and the *Journal of Digestive Diseases*. The second source is studies by research psychologists and psychiatrists. Here again we obtained our information from journals of psychiatry and clinical psychology. The third source is the theory and practice of folk medicine. We have surveyed folk medicine practices throughout history for those solutions to eliminatory problems that have been most widely and effectively used. We have researched the world's literature on such practices through journals and books.

Our book is divided into three parts. Within each, we give you a little history of the problem. We present the results of scientific research as well as some of the more accepted and simpler folk medicine approaches. In Part I we tell you briefly about the gastrointestinal system, what it looks like and how it works. We feel that a solid scientific base will give you the confidence in your own ability to deal with your body, and to this end we help you understand as fully as possible how food is digested, how the feces are formed, how the eliminatory processes work, and how certain factors may alter the structure and composition of the feces.

Part I also deals with the psychology of elimination. We discuss general ways in which our emotions help or hinder our bowel movements. Although not every physical disorder can be cured by a psychiatrist or a TM session, we do acknowledge the tremendous importance of psychological states of being. We shall guide you toward a deeper understanding of your mind, your body, and their interrelationships.

Part II explains how to maintain a healthy gastrointestinal system. This includes proper diet, exercises, effective toilet postures and activities, and cleansing techniques. Aside from the proved effectiveness of certain medical treatments, there are particular solutions to regularity that curiously reappear throughout history and in peoples on opposite sides of the earth, and we have paid special attention to such solutions as being of universal significance, and thus of great use to us. Certain foods have been shown again and again to aid regularity; certain exercises are repeatedly prescribed by physicians and folk healers. In this part we present a compendium of techniques and aids to regularity, with our specific recommendations for their best use.

Part III deals with malfunctions of the eliminatory processes—their diagnoses and their causes, preventions and cures. These malfunctions come under five headings: constipation, diarrhea, flatulence, hemorrhoids, and the range of other bowel disorders, from anal itch to bowel cancer. We clarify the nature of each disorder so that you can take control of your own health and understand and prevent malfunction whenever possible. You will get a clear idea of which malfunctions can be treated by the knowledge you gain from this book, and which ones require a visit to your doctor.

Finally, we give an appendix of recipes and herbal formulae for natural laxatives, antigas agents, binding agents, and enema mixtures. We also include a reference list to books and articles related to the issues discussed in each chapter.

At various points in the book we discuss personal experiences that are relevant to an understanding of the issues. As it turned out, George Wolf was of service in the preliminary researching of physiological data, and in the final editing. David Ehrlich researched and wrote the major portion of the book. We are indebted to David Kauffman, M.D., of Elizabeth, New Jersey, for his incisive criticisms of our flatulence chapter; to Peter Albright, M.D., of St. Johnsbury, Vermont, for his criticisms of the entire book; and to Kimberly Madore and Marcela Ehrlich for their aid in researching the medical articles.

We close this Introduction with a word of caution that we shall repeat in various forms throughout the book: *we do not intend this book to be a substitute for a physician, but only to serve as an adjunct to his work.* If you have persisting or intense symptoms that do not clear up with the natural treatments given in this book, we strongly advise you to see your physician. He will be in possession of sophisticated chemical and microscopic tools of diagnosis, and he will have a fuller knowledge of general bodily functions. But in most instances, if you practice the proper hygienic principles which we give you in this book, you should gain a healthier psychological and emotional attitude toward your bowels in particular, a greater knowledge of your body in general, and as a result a longer, happier, and more vital life.

PART 1

Physiology and Psychology of the Gastrointestinal System

1
How the Gastrointestinal System Works

The Nature of the Digestive Tract

Your life depends on the ingestion, processing, and elimination of foods. Although this book is about elimination, it will be good for you to know something about the general operation of the digestive system.[1]

First, let's look at the parts of the system and then we can talk about how it works later. When food is swallowed, it enters a tube called the esophagus which connects the mouth and the stomach. At the bottom of the esophagus is a little valve-like apparatus which opens to allow the food to enter the stomach and then closes to prevent the food from being forced back up from the stomach. The stomach is like an elastic bag with an opening at the top where the esophagus enters and an opening at the bottom where the intestines begin. There is a second valve at the lower opening to control the amount of food leaving the stomach. The intestines are made up of the small intestine and the large intestine (which is usually called the colon). There are valves (constrictions) at the juncture between the small intestine and the colon, and at the end of the colon, the anus. The entire length of the intestines has a wall of muscle which can contract rhythmically to churn and propel food. The rhythmic contractions are called peristaltic waves and the phenomenon is called peristalsis.

What Happens to Food in the Tract

The process of digesting food begins in the mouth where the food is broken up into small fragments and mixed with saliva. Saliva does two things—it acts as a lubricant to aid in swallowing and getting the food to the stomach, and it also begins the process of breaking down carbohydrates into glucose. Some bodily functions such as chewing and swallowing (the first) and excreting (the last) are under voluntary control, which means under our direct, conscious control. Everything in between is automatic. However, just because it's automatic doesn't mean that your mind can't effect what happens—but more about that later.

After the food is mixed with saliva, broken apart, and swallowed, it is moved down the esophagus by waves of muscular contractions. Then the stomach does three things. First, it stores large amounts of food immediately after a meal. Second, it secretes substances which break down the food. Third, it mixes and churns the foods. Three components of food have to be broken down before they can be assimilated. These are the fats, carbohydrates, and proteins.

One of the substances which the stomach secretes is hydrochloric acid, which helps break down all three of the food components above. The stomach also secretes substances such as lipases which break down the fats, and pepsin which breaks down the proteins. By the time the stomach is finished working on the foods, they have been turned into a milky substance called chyme. Next, the valve between the stomach and the small intestine opens and the food is pushed into the small intestine. As the food moves along the small intestine, the process of breaking it down into ever smaller elements continues, and a new process begins—the transfer of the elements through the walls of the intestines.

The secretions which break down the food in the intestines come from the pancreas, which is a large gland behind the stomach, and the liver, which lies just to the right of the stomach. The pancreas secretes several substances which neutralize the acid secretions of the stomach, and also further break down the fats, carbohydrates, and proteins. The liver secretes bile, which is stored in the gall bladder and released into the small intestine after food enters the stomach. The bile does not directly take part in digestion, but it acts as a detergent—it helps the digestive secretions attack the fat.

All along the intestinal tract, mucus is secreted. The mucus does not help in digestion, but it coats the walls to prevent them from being irritated by the various secretions, and it acts as a lubricant. By the time the food has passed through the small intestine and has reached the colon, all the good nutrients, as well as some of the water and minerals, have been removed. Now we are approaching the main topic of this book, so let's look at what happens in the colon in a little more detail.

Understanding the Process of Elimination

About twenty ounces of partially digested matter enters the colon each day. About sixteen ounces of this is water and minerals which are absorbed into the bloodstream. The remaining fecal matter, usually in the form of a bolus, is stored until it is expelled. The fecal matter is mixed by means of contractions of the colon, and these contractions break it up into large segments. The contractions of the colon dig into the fecal matter and roll it over in much the same way one kneads dough for bread.

When the colon becomes overfilled, sudden strong peristaltic movements occur, one after the other. These are called mass movements, and they propel the fecal matter for long distances through the colon. This whole process lasts only a few moments.

The final region of the colon is called the rectum, and when the mass movements have pushed the feces into the rectum, a reflex called the defecation reflex is stimulated. The reflex is started because the pressure in the rectum excites certain nerves in its wall. These nerves send impulses to the spinal cord, which then sends messages back to the intestinal wall causing it to contract. This stage of defecation is automatic. However, the valve (or sphincter) at the anal opening is under voluntary control and can be relaxed or tightened at will. The defecation reflex cannot cause expulsion of the feces unless the sphincter is relaxed. If the sphincter is not relaxed, the reflex will die out after a few minutes and return some hours later. On the other hand, you can indirectly initiate the involuntary defecation reflex by tightening your abdominal muscles. This will put pressure on the walls of the rectum and get the reflex going. Usually, though, this doesn't work as effectively as the natural defecation reflex, which is meant to expel the waste product smoothly and gently.

Now let's look a bit more closely at the composition of the waste product.

The Nature of the Digestive Waste Product

There are many words we could use to describe the digestive waste product. Most of them carry pejorative connotations and are interchangeable with monosyllabic curses. For the weak-hearted, we wish we could dream up a nice little phrase such as "droppings" or "unnecessities." However, we wish neither to be cutesy nor to complicate the already unwieldy vocabulary. We have chosen, therefore, to use the medical terminology in this instance and simply to call the waste product *feces*.

Feces are composed of several elements: (1) the remnants of food that cannot be digested; (2) remnants which are normally digestible but which for one reason or another were not absorbed; (3) by-products of the fermentation and bacterial reactions which break down the food; (4) secretions of the intestines such as mucus and salts; (5) bacteria and parasites; and (6) the breakdown products of blood and tissue cells.

The form, color, and consistency of feces can vary greatly in healthy people. The form and consistency are attributable mainly to the amount of water in the feces. Vegetable foods make the feces soft and pulpy. A meat diet makes the feces firm, and they often appear as short separate lumps. For a mixed diet, the feces are cylindrical and of fairly firm consistency. Another factor which changes the consistency of the feces is the length of time they are stored in the colon. The longer they are stored, the more water is absorbed from them, and the harder and smaller they become. This often gives rise to constipation and straining at stool, with resultant hemorrhoids. At the other extreme from this small, hard stool is diarrhea, when the feces pass through the tract so rapidly that little or no water is absorbed and the feces are excreted as liquid. This can also be a source of irritation to the anus.

The characteristic brown color of the feces is due to a substance called bilirubin which is made up of debris from the blood and bile pigments. However, the color of the feces is also affected by the particular foods you eat. Meat darkens the color and vegetables generally lighten it. You have all seen how certain pigmented foods such as beets or berries can lend their color to the feces. When the feces remain in the colon for a long time, as with a case of constipation, the feces appear darker, but in this case it is only the surface that is darker.

The odors of feces are due to different natural bacteria and chemicals in the gastrointestinal tract. These can vary as your diet varies. For example, you may have noticed how onions, asparagus, garlic, or fish can change the smell. Heavy alcohol use can cause an extremely foul odor.

When you are eating a balanced diet in the normal three daily meals, the amount of feces you eliminate each day will vary anywhere from three to seven ounces. The more fiber you include in your diet—fruits, vegetables, and whole grains—the larger the amount of feces you will pass and the softer will be the consistency. The more concentrated foods you eat, such as meats, cheeses, or sugars, the smaller the quantity of feces you will pass, and the harder the consistency. Africans on a fiber-rich diet have been known to pass five to ten times the amount of feces that is "normal" for the average American.

The formation of feces does not stop when you stop eating. You will continue to excrete up to an ounce of feces daily even after many days of complete fasting. This is because you will be digesting excess fat stored in your body.

The frequency of bowel movements can also vary greatly in healthy individuals. Usually the more feces you form, the more frequently you will have bowel movements—so you can expect to have more bowel movements on a vegetable diet than on a meat diet. The average number of bowel movements for healthy people is one or two each day, but some people who are perfectly normal have bowel movements only twice or even once a week. On the other hand, some healthy people have up to four movements each day. Irregularity is not determined by the frequency or infrequency of movements. It is determined by definite changes in what has become regular *for you* as an individual, and in the ease and thoroughness of the movement when it does come. Simply put, if you have been moving your bowels once a week for your entire life and feel no discomfort (no headaches or lassitude) and you do not strain on the toilet, then you are perfectly regular—*for you*. If, on the other hand, you feel tired all week at work, are often bothered by dull headaches, and when you finally do sit down on the toilet, must heave and strain only to pass tiny, dark, hard feces, then no matter how long you have been this way, you are not regular. We hope that by reading this book you will become an expert on what is regular in your own personal terms, and that you will be able to maintain your inner balance as well as prevent bowel complaints.

2
The Psychology of Eliminatory Processes

In this chapter we deal with the connections between the functioning of the bowels and the functioning of the mind. Why are we elaborating on this connection? First, for the sake of completeness, to show the surprisingly broad ramifications of bowel processes in life. Second, and more important, to enable you to identify common personality characteristics in yourself which are associated with bowel problems. Self-knowledge is a source of strength and can enable you to make informed, intelligent decisions relevant to your physical and psychological health.

Psychoanalytic Theory Concerning the Bowels

According to psychoanalytic theory, personality development occurs in stages. There are three basic stages of early childhood which correspond roughly to the following ages:

>　*Oral Stage*—the first two years (ages 1–2)
>
>　*Anal Stage*—the second two years (ages 3–4)
>
>　*Phallic Stage*—the third two years (ages 5–6)

For the sake of simplicity and clarity we will permit ourselves to talk in terms of broad generalizations and to differentiate the various stages of development much more precisely and methodically than they usually occur in reality. Nevertheless, most psychoanalytic theorists agree that the sequence and the general issues are more or less as we state them in our brief discussion.[1]

In the Oral Stage, the newborn infant experiences the tension of hunger and the pleasure of food intake and stimulation of the mouth. Similarly, his experience of physical discomfort is generally followed by physical and sensual nurturance—being held, soothed, rocked, and warmed by his mother or father. The child initially feels no distance between himself and his environment, and it is through associating the release of tension and the gaining of pleasure with another person (usually the mother) that he learns about people other than himself. He learns how to trust other people and to depend on them for the satisfaction of his needs. The transition from a state of rage and frustration when he is hungry and cold and alone, to the state of profound happiness and satisfaction when the mother cares for him, is continually repeated. This positive reinforcement by the mother is absolutely critical and provides a foundation for all later attachments to other human beings.

From this stage of total helplessness and dependency, we move to the next epoch of child development, the so-called Anal State. The child begins to walk, to talk, thereby to express his needs and to develop his autonomy. As he asserts himself more as an individual, he develops his own personality with his own unique traits. He moves, at first tentatively, around the world of his immediate environment. He explores things with the utmost curiosity and continually seeks to test out his newly discovered abilities and sensory motor capacities. He is primarily concerned with feeling out his own limits as well as those of his parents' control over him. One of the main issues in the interaction of parent and child at this stage of development is that of autonomy and control.

What we are concerned with here is the particular expression of the issues of autonomy and control in the arena of the toilet. Along with the development of motor skills and language comes the acquisition of control over the sphincter muscles. You will remember that the sphincter muscles are situated at the anal opening and are under voluntary control. According to Freud, parental attention to toilet training and the child's physiological development of sphincter control are supplemented by a shift of the main erogenous zone from the mouth to the anus. During the first two years, the main issue for the child was feeding. Now, elimination comes to be the critical issue. The child experiences pleasurable sensations in elimination, in the retention of the feces, in the experience of control of the sphincter muscles. Furthermore, as part of toilet training the child receives reinforcement from the mother when she responds approvingly to his "appropriate toilet behavior." She admires and applauds his productions, and this gives him pride in himself and in his creativity. This reinforces and supports his continual growth in autonomy and self-control. Therefore, if all goes well during this very important stage of life, emerging from it we have a child who is assertive, proud, and self-sufficient.

Now, let's go back to the beginning of the Anal Stage and look at what very well might occur if all does not go well.

The initial experiences of toilet training can be frustrating, confusing, even frightening. The child may well find his parents' attitude toward his excrements entirely confusing. He knows the physiological pleasure of moving his bowels and is often praised by the parents for his wonderful production, and yet the parent shows this strange abhorrence of the product itself, especially if deposited in areas away from the toilet. Moreover, even when the product is placed in the toilet, the parent cannot wait to pull the shiny metal lever and flush his creation all away. To make matters worse, our industrial society has come up with a mechanical contraption that, when flushed, gives off a terrible roar heard only in the jungles that accompanies the tremendous rush of water that hurtles the production into a deep, dark cavern below somewhere. The child must sit very very carefully, for will he not slip and wind up there in the black hole along with his creation?

Not every self-respecting child will quietly sit there and heed the dictums of the parent who engages in this bizarre and contradictory behavior. He finds it especially difficult to toe the line when, for the first time in his wee little life, he sees that, lo and behold, he can exert his control over the destiny of himself and his creations. He soon learns that he can even control the emotions of his parents. He can make them smile by efforts directed into the toilet and he can elicit dismay and exasperation simply by holding back. For the first time the child finds himself in a position of control and in opposition to his parents. Because of this, many contemporary students of child development believe that the toilet is simply a natural arena for the working out of a much more basic issue—that of autonomy, self-control, aggression, and the testing of limits. Conflicts that the child has with his own impulses as well as conflicts he may have with his parents may be left unresolved at the end of this stage of development. If so, he will not be able to move on to subsequent stages of life and tackle their characteristic problems from a firm foundation of autonomy and self-control.

We all have experienced at one time or another moments at which we or those close to us fell apart and acted very much like a child. We may suddenly scream, throw something at the floor, smash a fist into the wall, cry uncontrollably, or, more to the point of this book, at the very least, *we might be upset to the point of diarrhea or to the point of its opposite, of holding ourselves in, like the stubborn child, in a bout of constipation.* We may very well become at such moments just like the child that we once were.

Up to a limit, such regressive behavior is not abnormal. Let's look at the characteristic traits of a "normal" "anal type" of person. The most outstanding characteristics are the so-called anal triad: *parsimony, orderliness,* and *obstinacy.* Psychoanalytic theory states that parsimony, or frugality, is just a continuation of the old anal habit of retention. This habit was originally motivated by one or both of two factors: first, the erogenous and symbolic pleasure of retaining the feces; and second, the primitive fear of losing a part of one's body.

Orderliness and obstinacy are closely related. Orderliness is an elaboration of the efforts of the child to obey the parents and to comply with their demands to order the toilet habits, and not to make a mess. Obstinacy expresses exactly the opposite trend. That is, it is the continuation of the tendency to rebel against the regulative demands of the parent.

The anal triad of character traits is closely associated with a variety of other behavioral predispositions which as a matter of fact can be very adaptive in our society. These predispositions include punctuality, propriety, tidiness, sobriety, obedience, and deference to authority. We find that anal people are extremely productive. Their particular anal traits serve as a framework for our highly organized and complex industrial societies. In most normal people, the manifestations of anality are subtle and inconspicuous. Anal people may impress us by their highly adaptive behavior and their successful lifestyles. They are often held out as exemplary models to be emulated. They do not display a great deal of emotion. Instead, their behavior is controlled and proper. They appear impeccably dressed and well groomed, although generally conservative. In some sense, they are rather resistant to influence and change. They like security and predictability in their lives, and they may therefore seem to lack spontaneity. Although this characterization of the "normal" anal type of personality is somewhat simplistic in its generalizing, it constitutes a set of traits upon which most psychoanalytical writers seem to agree.

If you recognize yourself in some of these characteristics, it is not unlikely that you are prey to some bowel irregularities or problems—most likely constipation and/or hemorrhoids. We have all heard the expression "tight-ass personality." This refers to the anal personality we have been describing. Such a person is tight, not only in character structure but in physical structure as well—especially in the sphincter muscles which function to hold in bowel movements in the same way that the constricted personality holds in emotions. Continual tightness of the sphincter muscles will cause irregularity.

The prolonged storage of feces in the colon will then lead to its hardening and the "anal" personality finds himself constipated. On the other hand, overconcern with regularity can conflict with natural body functions and rhythms. If, because of your intense concern for regularity and order, and your inflexible reluctance to adapt your organizational structure to the natural impulse of the defecation reflex, you often find yourself forcing a bowel movement, the chances are you will suffer from hemorrhoids.

We can think of two possible ways to deal with bowel problems associated with the anal personality. First, if your personality or bowel problems are very severe, you will probably profit from some form of psychotherapy. But chances are that your problems are not so serious as to warrant such a radical commitment. You might try to loosen up your general approach to life, to express your feelings more openly to other people as well as to yourself. You might try to become more flexible in adapting to novel situations. This in turn may serve to release your natural bodily mechanisms from the kind of tight controls that hamper their optimal functioning. This is really nothing more than trusting your body the way an athlete or a dancer does. An expression we have heard a number of times from practitioners would seem of value here: "Lighten up, don't tighten up."

You will say, "Oh, it's all very well to say that, but in actuality, how does one do such a thing?" Well, in a sense, you utilize the very sense of rigidity and inflexibility that makes life so difficult for you. You use your refined sense of determination and perseverance to practice proved ways of loosening up your body and mind. Now, your fantastic reservoir of energy may be placed into instituting positive measures to loosen that system.

In Chapter 3, we tell you what foods and food combinations are best for smooth and healthful workings of your system. It may be that you will enjoy making lists of things to eat and not to eat, and that you will derive great calm and satisfaction from following the diets you have adapted from our suggestions. A healthful change in diet will go a long way toward improving the rigidities of your intestinal system, and may very well also lead to improvements in your general attitudes toward life.

In Chapter 4, we describe several programs of light and enjoyable physical exercise that will harmonize and smooth out your body functions. Abdominal muscle tone can be improved, and a sense of physical well-being will result that will tend to lessen the need for excessive self-control.

In Chapter 5, we give you some specific ideas on things to do on the toilet to release tension and alter associations from disturbing ones to happy ones.

Finally, we want to mention one more complicated issue. Many emotional and behavioral problems are transmitted from generation to generation because of the repetition of childrearing practices. Now that we have pointed out for you some of the relationships between toilet training and later personality and bowel problems, you can use this information to develop the most beneficial kind of relationship to your own children when they pass through the critical anal phase. Obviously, this is a period when a great demand is placed on your empathic attention to your child's feelings. You are called upon to be extremely patient, tolerant, and self-restrained. Most authorities now believe that a few more months of such tolerance will ultimately spare both you and your child a lot of unnecessary difficulties later on in life. So wait until your child shows you that he is interested in developing bowel control. Then you can guide him with understanding and encouragement while he moves along at his own pace.

Scientific Views on How the Mind and the Body Affect Each Other in Relation to Bowel Problems

Psychoanalytic writers laid the theoretical groundwork for modern scientific research on ways in which our emotions may influence our bowel functions. Recent studies have begun to explore the connections between particular disorders of the eliminatory tract and particular personality characteristics. We shall present a few examples of recent research and shall then take for granted a basic understanding of these principles in our discussions throughout the rest of the book.

A group of researchers at the University of Utah Medical School studied children who had continual problems of diarrhea, and compared them to children who didn't suffer from these problems.[2] The researchers found behavioral characteristics in children with diarrhea that were not found in the normal group of children. Moreover, these differences were apparent long before the problem of diarrhea had come to their attention. The children with diarrhea tended to be more emotional and less affectionate. Their sleep habits were more irregular, and in addition, they showed physiological problems such as digestive disorders. Their behavioral and physiological profiles as well as their emotional and personality patterns *both* pointed to a common disorder of the brain. The authors concluded, "It may be that chronic non-specific diarrhea and irritable colon syndrome occur in association with certain temperamental traits."

Other workers studying diarrhea in children looked at the *immediate* causes of the bowel disturbance rather than at the general relationship between personality and the disorder. In other words, what is it in particular that triggers an episode of diarrhea in these children? They found that there was a significant relationship between the occurrence of emotional conflicts between the parents and episodes of diarrhea. They statistically proved something, in fact, that all of us have considered at one time or another, that sometimes diarrhea is just a simple case of fear and anxiety, or a "fear and trembling" of the bowels.

Two British researchers found a strong connection between constipation and the inability to be flexible and change decisions.[3] Their report gives credence to the psychoanalytic theory that constipation often occurs in anal-type personalities.

A group of Boston researchers studied ulcerative colitis with regard to the personality traits associated with the disease. They concluded that the patients had subnormal autonomy.[4] You will remember that problems of autonomy were closely related to toilet training in the Anal Stage. These patients appeared fixated on infantile problems with parental authority, were extremely dependent on parental approval and protection, and were rather submissive and obedient. The medical research does not yet tell us *why* such a personality style is associated with colitis, only that it is.

More and more scientists are finding such correlations.[5] As the data unfold in the future, it will become clearer precisely what is causing what, and that will provide the knowledge to prevent physical disorders that are psychosomatic. As we continue through this book, we continually make note of the fact that medical practitioners are less inhibited than in the past about calling such disorders as flatulence and constipation psychosomatic or functional. And many practitioners also go so far as to state that the majority of cases of diarrhea and hemorrhoids are also nervous disorders.

The emotional connection to bowel disorders is no secret to folk healers throughout the ages. Many of the same herbal remedies given to soothe a nervous stomach or bowel are also prescribed to soothe a nervous mind or to cure insomnia. And so many of the "cures" for bowel complaints in primitive societies are magical, or placebo-effect cures, that one would be led to believe that the shamans and witch doctors knew as well as we do now that the mind can have as much effect on our bowels as can our eating habits. Folk healers as well as traditional medicine up to the Age of Reason were holistic. They treated the entire person, not merely a weak bowel or a single hemorrhoid. The treatment was addressed to the patient's mind and heart as well, with account taken of daily habits and problems that could be enough out of the ordinary as to be an effect on the disorder. Modern-day medicine allows for the bedside manner, and isn't this a bit of the same thing? Unfortunately, however, in the last twenty years the housecall has become a rarity and the physician's only opportunity for bedside manner is by the hospital bed, "on the run" from one floor to the other. Alas, with the sad decline of doctors who treat the whole patient has come the rise of the multitude of schools of psychological therapy which treat that sphere left by the abdication of the medical practitioner.

We fully hope that one of the effects of reading this book will be to get you to think of yourself as a whole person, not just as an isolated bowel. You have digestive and eliminatory organs, to be sure, but you have sphincter muscles that aid or hinder your functions, you have legs that if used in walking and in exercising will help your elimination as well as your entire system. You have a mouth for eating and chewing. You have feelings, emotions, that if pent-up inside you may lead to constipation, and if you are given to nervousness may lead to diarrhea. You have daily rhythms, schedules, which if too rigid will lead to constipation and hemorrhoids, and you have free choice over all things to do with your time, on the toilet or away from it, things that can either relax you or tighten you.

You, your mind and your feelings, have as much to say about your regularity as do those uncontrollable organs inside you, or the doctor outside you. You must be the one to take charge of your body, to guide it, flow with it when necessary, but most of all, to understand it and be at one with it.

In the following chapters we offer suggestions on ways in which you can get to know your body, to join with it in harmonious equilibrium. We hope that you can now enter wholeheartedly and whole-bodily into the latter part of this book and can use the materials presented not only to bring your eliminatory system to top-notch condition, but also to develop your entire body identity in integration with your mind and your heart.

PART 2

How to Keep Your Eliminatory System in Top-notch Condition

3
YOUR DIET

The great proliferation of diet and health books in the past ten years has lessened the need for us to tell you all the general things you should now know about your diet, namely, that the typical Western feeling that "white is best" has been entirely discredited, not only in the realm of race, but also in the case of white sugar, white breads, white cakes, and white flours. The color white does not often appear naturally. To achieve it, something must be added or something must be taken out, and that is precisely where the trouble is. The full, natural color of whole sugar and whole grains, of *all* kinds, is dirty-looking, "un-American" brown. You should either learn to live with that fact, or continue to pursue unwholesome eating habits which will cause bowel complaints to develop, no matter what else you adapt from this book.

In much the same way, by now you are either getting your full complement of vitamins and minerals (from a full, balanced diet or from a mixture of diet and vitamin-mineral supplements) or you are still feeling weak, sluggish, and prone to every cold and flu that hits your area.

You are either cutting down on your eating of red meat, of saturated fats, creams, and cheeses, or you are totally pleased with the prospect of the increased risk of cancer and heart failure.

It is not within the province of this book to cover the old ground in these areas, or to reconvince you of what you have no doubt been told many times. Our task is simpler: we want to deal with those aspects of your diet that most *directly* affect your daily habits of elimination. Now, obviously, everything you eat is relevant to your intestines, and

21

we do advise you to get a general picture of the effects of diet on health, if you have not already done so. But in a single chapter such as this one, we have chosen to cover the specific recommendations that would *most* serve to prevent disorders of the intestinal tract and would, in fact, promote healthy and exhilarating functioning.

In the event that you are in a hurry and cannot read the whole chapter, we would like to summarize quickly what we are about to say. It can be put in a very short paragraph:

Add fiber to your diet in the form of whole grains, whole flours, breads, cereals, whole pasta. Add fiber to your diet in the form of raw and cooked vegetables, and add both fiber and pectin in the form of *raw*, juicy fruits such as papaya, pineapple, apples, figs, bananas, etc. Eat water-absorbing, sponge-activity foods like seaweed and agar-agar. Cut down on sugar and syrup and eat plenty of raw honey. Eat lactic-acid products such as yogurt, buttermilk, sour milk, sauerkraut. Eat predigested vegetables such as sprouts. Cut down on meats, concentrated cheeses, sugars, canned and packaged powdered foods, spices, soda. Make sure you are getting plenty of vitamin B complex and vitamin A in addition to your other vitamins.

If you are one of those people who feels that after having gotten the simple rules there is simply no need to read the rest of the chapter, you are also the kind of person who bolts down your food without proper chewing. *This has been a test.* Slow down your reading of this book, extend your patience, for proper intellectual digestion. And, similarly, slow down your eating habits, chewing your food thoroughly and calmly.

Fiber

Throughout the last hundred years, there have been tremendous swings of opinion in relation to the benefits of fiber or "roughage." In 1886, in the noted medical journal *Lancet*, a physician wrote: "It is, I think, extremely doubtful if coarse food is useful in the long run. It causes atony and weariness of the muscles eventually by overstimulation."[1] In 1903, the noted French researcher De Langenhagen studied two thousand cases at the French watering place of Plombières and subsequently wrote, "It cannot be repeated too often that the food in muco-membranous colitis should be of a nature to leave as little residuum as possible for the inert intestine to get rid of."[2]

In the 1920s, this view was discredited and replaced by the idea that roughage was somehow advantageous.[3] Dr. Kellogg was one of the major proponents of this view, and the company in Battle Creek, Michigan, which bears his name set out to restore fiber, or cereals, to a place of eminence in the American diet. Then in the 1930s and 1940s, bland diets came back into vogue, and were replaced in the late 1960s by the present belief in the value of high-fiber diets.

Part of the confusion is no doubt due to semantics. The term "roughage" seems to imply that a coarse fiber much like an SOS pad, is grinding and sputtering away at the very tender surface of the intestines. Further, because it is popularly known that fiber is "indigestible," people who suffer from indigestion might be led to think that fiber would increase their problems. What really happens is that fiber, which is another name for the celluloses and polysaccharides of plant foods, is hydrophilic. This means that it draws water to itself and consequently makes the stool large, soft, and wet. Those of you who have a juicer might try an experiment. After you have juiced a few carrots, don't throw away the pulp, or carrot fiber, that remains in the top of the juicer. Place it in a bowl and add liquid to it, either water or a vegetable juice. The pulp will immediately swell up as it takes in the liquid. The resulting mass will be extremely soft, hardly deserving of the term "roughage." In fact, roughage might more appropriately be called "smoothage."

Why would scientists think that fiber would be beneficial to the system? The real story began in the late 1960s when Dr. D. P. Burkitt, who had spent a long time in Africa, gathered his findings and advanced an epidemiological hypothesis. If we find a particular disease that attacks society X more consistently than society Y, then it might be possible to explain the difference in terms of some deficiency in the diet of society X. Furthermore, if it can be proved that when individuals from society Y, who are free of the disease, tend to get it when they move to society X and adopt its dietary customs, we have even more reason to believe that there is a dietary deficiency in society X. If we further find that individuals in society X who do not prescribe to their society's diet tend to get the disease less frequently, then we have an even stronger case.

Burkitt opened up a hornet's nest with his comparison of the disease and dietary patterns of "primitive" Africans with those of so-called Westernized societies.[4] He found that the diseases of the colon, namely diverticular disease and colon cancer, were rare or unknown in peoples existing or subsisting on high-fiber diets. Furthermore, when Africans moved from their simple village life to a Westernized city, the incidence of colon disease increased. Other studies found that although incidence of colon disease in Western societies was greater than in African or Asian societies, it was much lower in particular groups living in Western society, such as Seventh-Day Adventists, Mormons, and Christian Scientists.[5] Burkitt contended that the primary dietary difference between Western and developing societies was related to the high proportions of animal or saturated fats and refined foods and low proportions of vegetable fiber in the Western diet.

As some researchers have pointed out, these epidemiological data are inconclusive.[6] The same societies of the West in which people eat more meat and less vegetables also produce more refined sugar, more industrial pollution, and more emotional stress. How can we know that the excess meat and the deficient fiber are the particular factors leading to greater incidence of colon disease?

Well, the studies by Burkitt and other epidemiologists were only a beginning. Since the late 1960s, when the theory came into vogue, there were a number of studies done on dietary changes in both animals and man, and although the data are not yet conclusive, scientists have found the following:

1. Cancer of the large bowel is linked to high animal fat intake.[7] Increase in dietary fat intake leads to a significant increase in fecal bile acid output. The precise role which fecal bile acids play in the development of bowel cancer has not yet been established, but a correlation has been shown, leading to speculation that they may even *enhance* tumor production.

2. Dietary fiber has an important role in preventing the excess buildup of these bile acids.[8] Persons taking adequate quantities

of natural fiber have bulkier stools, more rapid transit of the stools through the tract, and lower intracolonic pressures. The lowered pressures in turn decrease the possibility of both irritable colon and diverticular disease. The shorter transit time and more frequent bowel movements reduce the exposure time to bile acids or other carcinogenic material. Further, because of the greater bulk of the bowel contents, harmful materials may be diluted in some way and rendered less dangerous as they pass through the colon.

More simply stated, people who eat large quantities of saturated fats in the forms of meat, butter, and creams, either take in or produce an excessive amount of a potentially harmful substance in the intestines. Whether a person will then develop bowel cancer depends on a variety of elements, but one of the most important contributing causes may very well be infrequent and insufficient bowel movements. It might be possible to maintain a diet high in animal fats if one also eats large quantities of fibrous foods that would tend to dilute and more quickly and effectively carry out potential cancer-producing substances.

3. Most recently, studies in America have shown that there are chemicals in cruciferous plants (brussels sprouts, cabbage, turnips, cauliflower, and broccoli) which can reduce the number of tumor formations in rats.[9]

In 1978 Dr. L. W. Wattenberg, a researcher at the University of Minnesota, found that particular indoles occurring naturally in cruciferous vegetables can reduce the incidence of tumors in rats to one-fourth.[10] Epidemiological evidence shows that high intake of these vegetables by people is correlated with low incidence of cancer, and subsequently, low intake of the vegetables is associated with high incidence of cancer.[11] It seems likely that these vegetables offer protective mechanisms beyond their fibrous nature.

4. Recent studies have also shown that the beneficial effects of fiber, or bran, differ from food to food. A study reported in 1976 in the *American Journal of Clinical Nutrition* showed that the cereal-manufacturing process (which cooks the bran) alters wheat bran so that cooked bran has *less* effect on the intestines than

does a comparable amount of raw bran.[12] Raw bran increases the weight of the stool and causes faster intestinal transit than does cooked bran.

At first sight, it would seem to be quite simple for people to prevent serious bowel disease, and, moreover, aid their systems in maintaining regularity. They should eat less saturated animal fats and more fibrous foods in the form of raw bran and raw and cooked cruciferous vegetables. There have been several articles in recent years, however, which point out the difficulties in changing the eating habits of people even after it has been shown that those habits lead to increased risk of serious disease. One writer quotes Confucius, who said, "The essence of knowledge is, having acquired it, to apply it,"[13] Drs. Drasar and Hill, in their 1974 book *Human Intestinal Flora,* stated that even a halving of the daily fat intake to 50-60 grams per day would result in a much reduced and manageable fecal bile acid concentration.[14]

The addition of one ounce of raw bran daily to the diet would similarly be sufficient greatly to reduce the risk of serious and minor bowel disorder. And yet medical writers speak in terms of "the least changes in diet necessary to lead to a significant reduction in colon cancer."[15] It is extremely difficult to get an entire population to cut down significantly on its meat intake and to add fiber-rich foods. Besides the development of the taste for meat twice each day, Westerners view eating meat as a status symbol. The poor have meat once or twice a week when there is enough money saved for it. The rich have sirloin steak every day.

Many people, although they have read about the beneficial effects of bran, cannot develop a taste for its blandness. Further, bran still has the status of a food for "old people," to help their regularity, in much the same way prune juice does. There remains a bit of embarrassment in walking to the checkout counter with a box of bran.

Chances are, however, that if you are reading this book, you are not one of those embarrassed people. You have had the courage to walk up to the checkout counter of your bookstore with a book that obviously concerns bowel movements. You are concerned enough about your health to seek knowledge and, in most cases, as Confucius would say, "having acquired it, to apply it." We will even assume that you are health-conscious enough already to have cut down on your meat and saturated-fat intake, and that you are a connoisseur of vegetables. Some of you may even be vegetarians. And now, we have briefly given you more specific reasons for dietary change from what you most likely ate as a child to what you know you should be eating.

We have been speaking of prevention of serious bowel disease. This is extremely important. On the other hand, the less serious complaints of constipation and hemorrhoids should not be slighted. The same diet which prevents serious bowel disease also serves to prevent lesser disorders.[16]

Cutting down on meat intake and adding fibrous foods to the diet serves to establish regularity. The stools grow softer, bulkier, more cleansing, and more satisfying. Surely you have found that when you eat large quantities of meat your stools are smaller, harder, and more difficult to pass. And you have found that when you eat one of a variety of ethnic dishes rich in rice and vegetables, your stool the next day is softer and easier to pass.

Increase your use of raw bran. Add it to soups, to gravies, to salads, to juices, to cereals, to dishes of rice and spaghetti. One ounce each day will be just enough. Eat whole grains instead of the refined powders and meals that flood the supermarket shelves. If you haven't done so already, you will develop a real taste for whole-grain rice, buckwheat, and millet, as well as for the whole-grain breads. Eat plenty of raw and cooked vegetables, especially the cruciferous kind we have listed. And cut down on saturated fats even more than you have done. If you do these things, you will be contributing greatly to your health and regularity. We offer recipes for vegetable and grain dishes in Appendix A and we hope that you can learn to create your own dishes using fibrous foods, and that, after a few months of such dishes, your tastebuds will be repelled by even the thought of refined flours and fatty meats.

Garlic

For over five thousand years garlic has been used both as a food and as a healing agent. The Babylonians knew of its healing properties, and the Egyptians fed it daily to the slaves working on the pyramids. The

Chinese, Greeks, Romans, and Hindus of ancient times all claimed that garlic cured and prevented intestinal disorders such as constipation, diarrhea, and flatulence. A multitude of claims have been made on behalf of garlic. It has been said to cure snakebite, skin disease, respiratory infection, typhoid, and cholera, to name a few. For the purposes of our book, we wish only to mention garlic's use as an aid to the expulsion of gas, as a cleansing agent in the intestinal tract, and as a mild stimulant to a bowel movement. Garlic has remained the remedy most commonly prescribed by folk healers throughout history. Modern research has borne out earlier theories of the curative powers of garlic.[17] It seems to restore regularity to the eliminatory system, and to aid the body in controlling the number of intestinal parasites that often lead to bowel disorder such as diarrhea.

Taken regularly, garlic may aid in lessening stomach and intestinal ailments. The allicin in garlic stimulates the walls of the stomach and intestines, and promotes the secretion of digestive enzymes.

Garlic can be eaten raw, as it has been for centuries by Slavs in Russia and Bulgaria. It can be peeled, cut into tiny pieces, and dropped into a salad, as in parts of the Near East. It can be cut and cooked into breads, as in Italy, or into soups and main dishes, as in France and other parts of Europe. It can be pickled in vinegar or soy sauce, as in the Far East, made into garlic wine, as in Japan, or even freeze-dried, as it is in East Europe.

Taking garlic raw, with green vegetables such as parsley, tends to neutralize the powerful smell and make it more palatable for the average person. For those of you embarrassed by even the hint of a whiff before family and friends, there are garlic capsules and pills made with dried garlic powder alone or mixed with dried parsley powder. These pills have shown themselves to be especially helpful in cases of flatulence.

Some people with irritable colon may react negatively to garlic. If you are one of these people, check with your doctor before continuing to use it. In any event, you should take only small amounts, and combine it with other foods.

No matter in which form you prefer it, garlic is an invaluable aid to your digestive and eliminatory system. Learn how to use it and to enjoy it. We include recipes in Appendix A for a variety of dishes.

Yogurt and Soured-milk products

The Bible mentions yogurt several times. The Roman historian Pliny mentions that the Assyrians thought yogurt, or "lebeny," to be a divine food as well as a cure for many illnesses. Herodotus, the Greek historian, writes that the Tartars of Asia used to drink a fermented milk. Galen, the ancient Greek physician, wrote that yogurt was very beneficial for bilious and burning stomachs and that it changed their nature by purifying them. An ancient Arab medical expert, Maserdschavia, wrote that yogurt should be used for dysentery and all inflammatory diseases of the stomach, liver, and intestines, because it rids the body of poisons by destroying them.

Yogurt is known throughout the world by a variety of names, and is eaten both by itself and in combination with other foods. Many peoples in the Far East and Africa have deficiencies of lactase, which is needed to break down the lactose of milk. These people tend to get indigestion, flatulence, and possibly diarrhea, when they drink milk. In yogurt or soured milk, however, the lactose has already been broken down by fermentative bacteria producing large quantities of lactic acid. Even for those of us with no lactase deficiency, this acid acts as a tonic to the digestive tract, mildly and gently stimulating it, and helping to correct the balance between healthy digestive bacteria in the intestines and those potentially harmful but active bacteria that cannot so effectively develop in an acid medium.[18] It further serves in aiding the digestion of fibrous vegetables. In fact, for those of you who find it difficult to eat large quantities of raw vegetables without flatulence, yogurt dressings are the perfect answer.

When antibiotic drugs are given to patients in hospitals, nurses are aware that although putrefactive and harmful bacteria are destroyed, the beneficial digestive bacteria are also destroyed. When you are given yogurt in your hospital bed, it is because it helps to *restore* the normal population of digestive bacteria before other, harmful bacteria, immune to the drug, can make their appearance in the vacuum created.

All soured-milk products, such as yogurt, buttermilk, sour milk, kefir, as well as fermented vegetables such as pickles and sauerkraut and the Oriental pickled plums, have a lactic-acid effect on the intestines. Pickled garlic possesses the benefits of garlic as well as of lactic acid, and has been used for centuries by Orientals for its antibiotic as well as stimulative properties in the intestines. For a rough equivalent, try some raw garlic cut up into tiny pieces and mixed with yogurt.

By adding soured-milk products to your diet, you will be aiding in the prevention of flatulence and in the digestion of the fibrous foods we have advised you to eat. You will help your intestines maintain a healthy balance of bacteria and will help prevent both constipation and diarrhea. (We offer some delicious yogurt recipes in Appendix A.) We do wish to caution you about those yogurt concoctions sold in supermarkets in which 20 percent of the volume is a very sugary jam. The fact that you are eating 80 percent healthy yogurt should not blind you to the fact that you are eating a jam you would not otherwise eat. The jam is pure sugar, which, besides having no food value beyond the calories, may cause gas or a bit of irregularity to people who cannot well tolerate concentrated sugars.

Fruit

Apples

Apples, bananas, and other fruits contain a substance called pectin. This is a hydrophilic substance that takes up a large amount of water. It is sold powdered or made into a syrup and is used as a kind of gel for making fruits into jams and jellies. When we eat apples or bananas, the pectin content takes up water in the digestive tract and moves through the entire tract, gently drawing bacteria and other debris away from the intestinal walls. Aside from the absorptive qualities of the pectin, which are similar to those of grain fiber, there may also be a separate healing effect on the gastrointestinal tract which soothes irritated membranes and restores tone.[19]

Papaya

Papaya is often mentioned in the writings of the early explorers who found, much to their surprise, that natives could eat extremely heavy meals of large quantities of fish and meat with no stomach distress if the meals were followed or accompanied by papaya.

The unripe fruit of the papaya contains a protein-digesting enzyme called papain which resembles pepsin in its digestive action.[20] The papain is extracted from the papaya, dried, and made into both meat tenderizer and tablets used for protein digestion. Natives of tropical countries still use the unripe papaya as an aid to digestion of proteins, and papaya tablets are finding their way into more and more drugstores and health-food stores. The whole fruit is available in most parts of America and Britain, and is a delicious, welcome addition to a meal. It has all the advantages of other fruits, with the addition of the digestive aid, papain. It is especially delicious and effective when eaten with yogurt.

Pineapple

Pineapples contain a meat-digesting enzyme called bromelin, which is similar to papain. Unlike papain, however, which is found only in the unripe papaya fruit, bromelin is found in both the unripe and the ripe pineapple. This explains why pineapple juice cannot be made as a gelatin dessert. Gelatin is protein and is digested by the bromelin in the pineapple juice. There are many recipes, originating in the tropics, for pineapple to be cooked along with pork, beef, and chicken, for in this cooking the meat is tenderized and made more digestible. We have chosen not to offer meat recipes in this book, but we offer recipes for pineapple in combination with other fruits, and of course with yogurt.

Prunes

Prunes and prune juice have long been known to cure even the most stubborn cases of constipation. In addition to the pectin and fiber contained by most other fruits, prunes contain a substance called dihydroxyphenylisatin which seems to stimulate intestinal motility.[21] In fact, overeating prunes or prune juice will cause a definite case of diarrhea, *from overstimulation*. There are many ways to eat prunes. The most common ways are to stew them in water or to leave them in some water with a bit of lemon juice overnight. They are taken in the morning before breakfast, the liquid drunk first, and then the prunes eaten. Taken every morning or so, regularity should be assured.

Figs

Figs growing in Syria, Persia, and Asia Minor, have been valued since ancient times. The ancient Greeks considered them so valuable that they prohibited the export of the best trees from the land. Fig trees were introduced into England by the Romans, and they were brought to America in the eighteenth century by the Franciscan monks who built the early missions in California. In addition to their fiber and pectin, figs contain hundreds of tiny seeds which serve as a mild stimulant to the intestines. They are eaten like prunes—stewed or soaked overnight. Soaked figs and prunes are delicious and extremely effective in maintaining regularity when eaten in combination with yogurt.

Honey

Paleontological investigations show that there were bees in the Tertiary Period, fifty-six million years before the appearance of man. The oldest reference to the gathering of wild honey is the New Stone Age wall painting in Spider Cave near Valencia, Spain. It depicts a human figure taking honey from a hole in a cliff with bees circling around in typical menacing fashion. The most ancient medical papyrus of Egypt, written about thirty-five hundred years ago, says that honey should be used to induce urination and ease the bowels. In ancient India, people attributed to honey many curative and tonic properties such as intestinal cleansing. In ancient Greece, Homer sang praises to honey, and Pythagoras, the father of mathematics, said that he had lived to be ninety because of eating honey. Democritus, who developed the atomic theory; Hippocrates, the father of medicine; and Aristotle—all advocated honey as a means of health and longevity. The Greek scientist Dioscorides wrote that honey could be effectively used against intestinal disease, and Galen, the famous Greek physician, also advocated the use of honey for intestinal disorder.

For thousands of years folk healers throughout the world have recommended honey as an aid to digestion and as a preventative in constipation, diarrhea, and intestinal disorders. Medical and biological research carried out extensively in Russia and Eastern European countries (most notably at the Bee Research Center in Bucharest,

Roumania) has shown that a diet rich in honey decreases acidity in patients with high gastric acidity, such as in cases of gastric and duodenal ulcers. In people with digestive difficulties, honey is quickly absorbed and acts as a mild stimulant to digestion. It soothes the mucous membranes of the intestinal tract, and is reported to serve as a mild antibiotic against putrefactive bacteria.[22]

Honey may be eaten raw, right from the comb, as the proverbial bear does. The most beneficial effect on the intestinal tract, however, seems to be from honey dissoved in warm or hot water. Thus diluted, it is more easily absorbed. It can be added to all teas and hot drinks in place of sugar, and makes a wonderful dish out of yogurt or sour milk. In fact, in the Middle East honey with yogurt is very popular, as is honey in combination with sesame butter (tahini) in a well-known dish called halvah. Ancient Palestine was called the Land of Milk and Honey in the Bible, and honey mixed with warm milk or buttermilk at bedtime is an excellent calming drink on the nervous system as well as on the entire digestive system. Honey should become a staple in your diet. Eat it in place of sugar. Include it in all your recipes for cakes and cookies and other desserts. Use it on your breads and toast slices instead of jam, and use it to sweeten fruits like grapefruit and berries. An ounce of honey each day, used in these ways, should be of inestimable value in establishing and maintaining regularity. And at times of unavoidable intestinal disorder, honey can serve as an additional curative agent.

There are literally thousands of honeys, made by bees throughout the world, from hundreds of thousands of various flowers, plants, and trees. Specialty shops and health-food stores stock a variety of honeys from different parts of the world, each with its own distinct aroma and flavor. We cannot think of any other food more susceptible to connoisseurship than honey. It is cleansing, stimulating, and delicious. What more could you ask for?

Seaweed

Seaweed has been used in the Orient for thousands of years as both a nutritious food and also as a healing agent. There are many varieties of seaweed, as many as there are land plants. In the West, they have all been grouped into one category and called kelp, but we hope that in the future greater use of this valuable food will lead to a more developed differentiation among the various types. Apart from its tremendous supply of vitamins and minerals, and its extremely high iodine content, seaweed offers excellent bulk for the intestines. It is hydrophilic in that it draws in and retains water. Just take some dry seaweed and whisk it under a running faucet for a few seconds and see how quickly it sponges up the liquid!

One type of seaweed, agar-agar, is similar in effect to fruit pectin and is often used along with it in creating gels of various kinds. It forms a smooth, slippery bulk in the intestinal tract and acts as a natural regulator of the bowels. Agar is sold in some supermarkets, health-food stores and in all Oriental food stores, in either powdered form or in small dried cubes. It may also be dissolved in soups or sauces to thicken the liquid into a gel.

Seaweed may be eaten in various ways. It is usually sold dried, either powdered or whole. If powdered, it can be sprinkled on salads or into soups, sauces, or juices like salt. If whole, it can be cut up and added to soups and vegetable stews like dried vegetables. Or it can be soaked for a few moments to regain its soft natural quality and added just like any other vegetable. In the Orient it is fried in batter for tempura, or baked in dough for a kind of salty cracker. We offer several recipes in Appendix A for this delicious, health-giving vegetable. We hope it will be used more often in the West.

Sprouts

An ancient Chinese medical text, the *Shen Nung Pen Ts'ao King*, compiled about A.D. 500 by T'ao Hung King, recommends adding bean sprouts to the diet for a number of maladies, chief among which were a group of digestive disorders. In the late sixteenth century, Li Shih Chen wrote the *Pen Ts'ao Kang Mu*, one of the greatest Chinese pharmaceutical natural histories. It lists soybean sprouts as possessing laxative properties and reducing inflammation. Mung bean sprouts were said to counteract the effects of alcohol, and sprouted barley (malt) was said to be peptic and demulcent (soothing to the intestinal walls).

Sprouted grains and seeds have been used for thousands of years in the Far East. They offer an alternative to fresh vegetables, in places and at times that fresh vegetables would not ordinarily be found. A traveler moving across Manchuria might take a handful of seeds from his pocket, soak them, and germinate them into nutritious sprouts in but a few days. The West used them at different times on board naval vessels to prevent scurvy or vitamin C deficiency. But for the most part, only Orientals have developed the use of sprouts.

During World War II, sprouted grains were suggested as possible antiscorbutics when the blockade of the British merchant marine led to potential shortages of fresh citrus fruits, but the suggestion was not followed up by action. In the United States, the Emergency Food Commission, which expected a protein shortage by 1944, suggested an alternative protein source from sprouted soybeans. In 1943, as part of a publicity campaign to educate the public about making and eating soybean sprouts, Governor Dewey of New York gave a huge banquet, serving only soybean and soybean-sprout courses. A multitude of magazines and journals followed up by extolling the virtues of sprouted seeds and grains. The anticipated shortage of protein never occurred, however, and by 1945 soybean sprouts became a discredited thing of the deprived, rationed past.

In the past ten years, however, sprouts have become a cause célèbre among health-food fans, and mung, soy, and alfalfa sprouts slowly found their way into supermarket chains until now in the 1980s, they seem to be as popular and as well known as brussels sprouts.

The sprouting, or germination, of any seed is always accompanied by a powerful enzymatic hydrolysis of protein. Stored proteins are broken down into their component amino acids, similar to the state of bodily digestion of the protein. Because they are already, in part, digested by the enzymes, the sprouts are more easily assimilated than the original beans or seeds. There is less indigestion and less flatulence. Besides the increased digestibility of the sprout over the original seed, there is a large increase of vitamin C, vitamin E, vitamin K, and carotene, as well as of protein content, which may increase up to 40 percent.

The most successful sprouts for eating are from the Leguminoseae family (peas, chick peas, beans, fenugreek, alfalfa, clover, lentils, and soybeans), the Granineae family (wheat, rye, corn, barley, millet, and oats), and the Cruciferae family (mustard, radish, cress, and kale). And you can fill your refrigerator with a variety of different kinds of sprouts. We offer recipes, as usual, in Appendix A. Most people find sprouts delicious in salads or mixed with yogurt and garlic for a wonderful, easily digestible tonic to the eliminatory system. Add them generously to your diet and enjoy their fresh, crunchy taste.[23]

Vitamins

There are countless books sold in health-food stores and drugstores extolling the virtues of the vitamin counter. We have counted well over a hundred possible vitamin and mineral supplements you could buy if you had a mind to do so. This book does not attempt to deal with so vast an issue. If you modulate your diet so that you increase your intake of raw fruits and vegetables and whole grains, as well as yogurt and sour-milk products, sprouts, and seaweed, it is possible that you would never need a vitamin supplement. On the other hand, how many of us really maintain a consistently balanced and reasonable diet? For the majority of us, some kind of minimum vitamin supplement may be advisable, and with that in mind we briefly list a few of the more important supplements, those especially necessary to the well-being of the eliminatory system:

1. *Vitamin A* is required for healthy maintenance of the mucus membrane of the entire colon, Without it, the mucus surface deteriorates and becomes sensitive, spongy, and ulcerated. A teaspoon of cod liver oil every morning will fulfill your need for vitamin A in addition to acting as a gentle stimulant and lubricant to your intestines. If you cannot stand the taste, you should take one 20,000-i.u. capsule of vitamin A each morning before breakfast.

2. *Vitamin B Complex* regulates the action of the bowels and has a beneficial effect on digestion, helping to eliminate flatulence and stomach pains. Whole grains and unrefined flours contain ample amounts of B vitamins. If you've been eating refined grains and breads for a while, or if you don't eat whole grains

every day, you might do well to take a B-complex vitamin supplement in the morning and in the evening. As an alternative,
brewer's yeast and wheat germ, as well as soya beans, contain
large amounts of B vitamins. These foods are especially beneficial
to regularity and to the well-being of your intestinal tract, as well
as to your entire body and mind.

3. *Calcium and magnesium* are of value in soothing the intestinal muscles, especially in more serious cases of colitis in which
spasms may occur. Dolomite powder or capsules, containing a
natural combination of calcium and magnesium, may be taken
in moderate amounts.

The Process of Eating

Chewing

No chapter on diet would be complete without a mild exhortation to
chew your food well. "Fletcherism" was popular at the turn of the
century. This way to optimal health called for the mastication of every
morsel of food at least a hundred times. How silly this seems in light of
the lunch-on-the-run. This is something for south-of-the-border
peoples who take three-hour siesta breaks for lunch! Everyone knows a
Big Mac can be chewed in three bites!

In a certain sense, we need not even chew the hamburger once. It
can be swallowed whole and broken up and digested in our stomach.
On the other hand, why give our digestive organs so much work to do?
Why not help them out as much as possible by masticating our food
thoroughly. In addition to our teeth's breaking up food into tiny particles, the ptyalin in our saliva serves initially to break down carbohydrates so that by the time the hamburger and bun reach our stomachs,
the bun has already been initially acted on by the enzymes in our
saliva. Our digestive organs can now concentrate on the more serious
effort of breaking apart the amino acids and fats in the hamburger.
There is a third benefit to thorough mastication. It slows down the
intake of food so that it can be more easily handled by our systems, and
the slow chewing tends also to reduce the chances of excessive taking

in and swallowing of air while eating, which cause aerophagia and flatulence. You need not chew each mouthful a hundred times, but you should nevertheless chew "thoroughly."

Relaxed Atmosphere

It cannot be emphasized too much that a friendly, relaxed atmosphere is indispensable to proper digestion of our meals. Eating while nervous or angry will cause excessive secretion of gastric acids, swallowing air, potential spasms of the digestive tract, and will undoubtedly lead to a good case of indigestion, heartburn, gas, and one of the various "pains in the ass." Mealtime should be a warm and meditative experience. The table should be attractively set, the food pleasingly arranged and prepared for all the senses: visual and olefatory as well as gustatory. The Japanese ritual of eating, which constitutes a meditative multimedia performance, replete with visual display of food and participatory ceremony, is a perfect example of an atmosphere conducive to the most harmonious eating and digestion. Those of you who use your dinner fork as a debating tool with which to dissect your opponent, or those of you who are parents who like to use mealtimes to discipline children, take note: emotional excitement will take its toll later. Relax and enjoy a fine meal.

Overeating

Compulsive eating is as much a sickness as is alcoholism or drug addiction. Compulsive eaters begin a meal thinking they will have a particular portion of food. When the portion is finished, they continue to dish out seconds onto their plates and eat and eat and eat. Then after the serving plate is emptied, they journey on to the refrigerator to "see what's left for tomorrow" and end up tasting it down to the last little piece. A compulsion has taken control of them and they are, in a sense, no longer responsible for their eating.

The way to avoid this is simple. Prepare only the quantity of food to suit precalculated meal needs. Do *not* make enough for the next day. When that quantity is finished, you are finished eating. If there are others living with you, ask them to help you by gently but firmly admonishing you to refrain as you tiptoe to the refrigerator. Some success has even been reported with a lock and key on the refrigerator, although compulsive eaters have shown themselves to be remarkably adept at wheedling keys by outpourings of felt deprivation. This is really a problem for another book. Suffice to say here that overeating causes flatulence or indigestion, and leads alternately to constipation and diarrhea. No system can withstand such an onslaught for long.

Conclusion

As we said at the outset of this chapter, everything we had to tell you about diet could be summed up in a short paragraph. We have decided to end the chapter with a similar list, a kind of checklist from which you might check off those items that are gradually integrated into your daily diet.

Benjamin Franklin was one of the most famous and dedicated proponents of the checklist. When Franklin arrived at the French court as the first American ambassador, he realized that his manners were sufficiently different from those of the court to cause embarrassment, and so, in typical well-organized fashion, he set about to change his behavior. He wrote down a list of all traits he considered boorish and forced himself to check off each one daily if acted upon. It so pained him to see himself check off these traits that he conditioned himself to avoid them, and in so avoiding them, to end them. Or at least all of them but two, which he had never intended to end—wearing his coonskin cap, which was his trademark, and his lechery, which was his joy.

The list we present to you is more in the manner of those kindergarten charts which give you a gold star for every book you've read. We'd like to see you end up with daily checkmarks in at least three-quarters of the items listed. Let's see how you do.

1. Eat one ounce of raw bran daily, combined with other foods or eaten alone.
2. Eat at least one full serving of a whole-grain dish or whole-grain bread.
3. Do not eat any refined white bread, flour, cake, or pasta.

4. Eat at least two daily servings of raw or cooked vegetables, including one serving of a cruciferous vegetable such as cabbage, brussels sprouts, etc.

5. If you are a meat eater, cut your intake to two ounces daily, average.

6. Have the equivalent of at least one garlic clove daily.

7. Eat at least one pint of yogurt or other sour-milk product daily.

8. Eat at least one pound of raw fruit every day, such as apples, bananas, papaya, pineapple, figs, prunes.

9. Eat at least an ounce of honey every day, mixed with yogurt or milk, or used as a sweetener in warm tea at bedtime.

10. Include one ounce, dry weight, of seaweed in salad or vegetable or grain dish every day.

11. Eat at least two ounces of fresh sprouts every day.

12. Take a teaspoon of cod liver oil, or one 20,000-i.u. dose of vitamin A every morning.

13. Take B complex tablets, or take at least three tablespoons of wheat germ or brewer's yeast daily.

14. Chew each mouthful between five and ten times.

15. Do not allow yourself to be emotionally upset during or after meals.

16. Do not overeat.

4
Exercising for Better Bowel Function

Walking

We have found that of all the various forms of exercise you may perform, walking is such a natural and enjoyable pastime that you will have great success in developing a liking for it and in consistently carrying through on it as time goes on.[1]

Most of us wake, sit down for breakfast, take the car, train, or subway to work while again sitting, then spend the entire day sitting behind a desk or on a tractor, except for brief periods for lunch and coffee break, when we again sit. At the end of the day, we sit as our vehicle takes us home to eat, watch TV, or read a newspaper, all of which varies only in the style of chair on which we sit. Is it any wonder then that when we sit on the toilet, our abdominal muscles have become so inactive as to seem "estranged" from us when they are called on to perform?[2] When you walk, you are increasing your circulation, gently strengthening your heart, and exercising your abdominal muscles, all of which are important in the bowel movement.

Think of all the times in the past you have chosen or have been forced to walk, and try to remember the times you really and truly enjoyed it. Easiest to remember will be those walks along Champs-Élysées in Paris, if you had the luck. Certainly these are experiences anyone would treasure. Now, think a bit further, about moments not quite so spectacular. Think of the time that your car was in the repair shop and you took that walk home from work at sunset. Think of the time you just happened to find yourself in the neighborhood you grew up in and you walked around a bit to get the old feelings back. Think of walks with a person you have loved. Think of walks alone when you were joyful, and when you were sad as well. There is something very special that happens on walks, something unlike most of our other experiences, something that brings us a little closer to a deeper part of ourselves.

As with all exercises, you should begin slowly, gradually. Perhaps your next vacation will give you the best opportunity to get your legs moving. If you don't have the time or money for a vacation, why not walk a few blocks tonight to the drugstore to get your evening paper. Or instead of going downstairs for lunch in the same building in which you work ("because you have no time"), take the full lunch hour and walk over to the park with a packaged lunch. Or if you must eat at a restaurant, walk over to that new one six blocks away. In the morning, walk a few blocks more to the next subway stop, or you may even awaken an hour earlier and walk to work (assuming you are not a commuter). Do you grow frustrated when the elevator overlooks your buzzer and passes you by? You'd be surprised how easy it will be to climb a few flights of stairs once you've started walking.

Depending on your schedule, you should try to get in a nice walk just before the time you usually have a bowel movement. With many people, this is in the morning right after breakfast. For most people, the introduction of food into the digestive tract upon awakening stimulates the defecation reflex. If this has generally been the case with you, you might consider waking a bit earlier, having a tall glass of water, fruit juice, herbal tea, yogurt, or buttermilk, and going for a half-hour walk. Have you ever awakened before 6:00 A.M. and taken a walk in a large city? The streets are fresh, quiet, and peaceful. You may even hear the birds! Perhaps this will prove to be such a rewarding experience that you find yourself beginning to repeat it again and again. Many people find this time best for quiet meditation on yesterday and planning for today. This will be the perfect exercise and state of mind for the effective and fulfilling bowel movement. Your circulation and abdominal muscles will have awakened to a vibrant stimulation, and the relaxed ambience of your walk will be most conducive to the "strainless movement." The tall glass of liquid is just what your digestive system needs to wake up and prepare the feces for utmost motility. After you walk, you may find that you can go straight to the toilet before breakfast. Or, like most people, you first sit down to breakfast, invigorated by your walk, and afterward, *because you have still left yourself an adequate period of time without rushing,* you sit down to a full and thorough movement.

Abdominal Muscle Exercises

Specific kinds of exercises are helpful when done consistently over a period of time. To do them for a week and then stop will bring a tightness and mild physical depression. If you are constipated, your irritation at yourself may be just enough motivation to begin a rigorous series of exercises. But chances are that after following one or more of the recommendations in this book, your constipation will cease. At that point, if your exercises are not fulfilling in other ways, you will no longer feel the need for them and you will begin to procrastinate in performing them until your abdominal muscles again grow lax. If you have found that you are not the "exercise type," simply place your energies into walking, which can be such a pure pleasure that, integrated into your lifestyle, it can remain a part of your life even after you feel you no longer need it to improve your bowel function. On the other hand, for those of you who enjoy exercising, or who are simply curious about your reactions, we offer helpful abdominal exercises. Remember, begin in moderation and *gradually* build both in intensity and in the amount of time devoted to the exercises, lest you either strain your muscles or overdiscipline yourself into a distaste for all exercise.

    1. Lie on your back, hands behind your head. Either hook your feet under a heavy chair or have someone sit across your ankles. Raise your body to a sitting position. Then *slowly* lower yourself. This should be repeated five times every morning for a week. The second week, you should begin to increase the number of

sit-ups: six the first day, seven the second day, eight the third, and so on until you begin to feel strained.

2. Lie on your back, arms out to the side and raise your left leg slowly without bending the knee. Then slowly lower it to the ground. Slowly raise your right leg, again without bending your knee, and slowly lower it. Repeat the exercise five times. Gradually increase the number of leg-raisings each week. Do not push yourself to the point of strain.

3. Go out to the country in the fall and pick apples off the ground. Pick dandelions. Pick tiny pieces of lint off the floor with your fingers instead of the vacuum cleaner. Search for brightly colored leaves or interesting stones that you can arrange beside the fireplace. In other words, find excuses to touch your toes as much as possible. *With knees unbent,* bend down and touch your fingertips to the ground in front of you, first one hand, then the other, then both hands at once. As you do this, contract your abdomen, tighten it for a few seconds, and then release it. Tighten again and release. These contraction-release exercises are especially effective when done while toe-touching. And, of course, if you can find pleasant ways to integrate the exercises into positive aspects of your life, you will have a much better chance of making them permanent.

Yoga

For hundreds of years, people in the Orient have found the body and breathing exercises of yoga especially beneficial in the prevention of constipation and flatulence as well as conducive to the well-being of the entire body. We could very well write a whole book on all the various exercises that would be of value to you in your bowel movements, because any exercise that benefits your balance, harmony, and sense of well-being will most certainly influence the equilibrium of your eliminatory system. We have, however, limited this section to those few exercises we have found most directly beneficial to your eliminatory system in the hopes that once these exercises are begun, you will also investigate the variety of other modalities available nationwide in yoga classes and workshops.[3]

1. *Knee to Chest.* This exercise strengthens and tones the abdominal muscles as well as the digestive and eliminatory organs. Lie down on your back. Grasping your right knee with both hands, pull it firmly back so that it rests against your chest, with the thigh against your abdomen. Slowly inhale and then exhale, while lifting your head so that your forehead rests against your knee. Hold this position for a few moments, then release your body to the original flat position. Rest a few moments and then repeat with your left knee. As your body gradually loosens up through exercises, you can increase the number of times you do this exercise to three times for each knee.

2. *Yoga Mudra.* This exercise helps relieve both tension and constipation. Sit in a comfortable position. Put your arms behind you, straightening them in a horizontal position with hands clasped together. Slowly raise your chin up while inhaling through your nose as slowly as you can. Then slowly lower your head to the floor while exhaling. Slowly return to your original position while inhaling. Exhale.

3. *Abdominal Contraction.* Practiced on an empty stomach, this exercise will improve the waistline as well as the abdominal muscles and digestive system. Stand erect, hands at your sides, and inhale deeply. Then bend a bit forward at the waist, hands on thighs, and forcefully exhale all the air in your lungs. Hold for as long as you possibly can until you must take in air. Then release, stand up straight, and relax. Do these exercises *slowly* and do not overdo them for a couple of weeks.

The following exercises place less stress on physical exertion and more emphasis on breathing. They aid in relieving flatulence, in strengthening the abdominal muscles, and in stimulating the defecation response in some people. Other related and helpful effects of the exercises are cleansing lung tissue, nourishing red corpuscles and brain cells, and an overall feeling of lightness and buoyancy. The exercises are moderate Western adaptations of Tibetan mantras.

1. Stand erect, feet twelve inches apart, with your arms turned inward and down in front of you so that the backs of your hands lie flat against each other. Slowly pull your arms up over your head, while keeping the backs of your hands together, and inhale. As your lungs improve through these exercises, you should have no trouble in slowing down this inhalation to at least ten seconds. When your arms are extended straight above your head, hold your breath as long as you can. Then slowly lower your arms (backs of hands still together) while exhaling, until you are back to your original position. Continue to exhale until you feel there is no more air in your lungs. Hold for as long as you can, then inhale while relaxing. Each week you should increase the number of these daily exercises: the first week once daily; the second week, twice; etc.

2. This exercise is extremely effective in expelling accumulated gas. Lie down on your back with knees bent, up in the air. Take a deep breath slowly, hold it a few seconds. Then *slowly* exhale. Even after you think you have fully exhaled, push out the remaining air a few more times. Hold your breath as long as you possibly can. Then again, slowly inhale. Hold it. Now slowly exhale again. When you have fully exhaled, with the palms of both hands gently knead your abdomen in clockwise circles the size of a silver dollar from the upper right bottom of your right ribcage across to the left and then down. When you have done this, relax and slowly inhale again. Hold it. Then *while* exhaling this time, massage your abdomen in the same way. You should be able to release the gas quite easily as you are both exhaling and massaging your abdomen down the left side. If this does not prove effective at first, continue with the exercises.

3. The following exercise has proved of value in preparing the digestive system for a meal. Lie on your back, with hands behind your head and legs outstretched. Slowly raise your left leg, toes outstretched, while inhaling. Hold your breath ten seconds, then lower the leg while exhaling. Then raise the right leg while inhaling and lower it while exhaling. Do this a few times. Then raise both legs, toes still stretched out, while inhaling, hold, then lower the legs slowly while exhaling. You should gradually increase the number of times you do the exercises until you are doing five repetitions of each one.

4. The following exercise is a good complement to your recommended walks. While walking, inhale through your nose in short staccato breaths. When you think you can take in nothing more, hold your breath for at least ten seconds. Then exhale in short breaths through your mouth. Many people have a bit of creative fun with this and develop staccato forms of singing, whistling, or other preverbal forms of expression. One might even work out rhythmic nostril percussion on the inhalations. In any event, remember to inhale and exhale as fully as possible, holding your breath after each step. And most important, enjoy your walk!

5. The following exercise will lead us right into the next chapter which concerns postures and positions on the toilet. It has proved effective in relieving constipation as well as the hemorrhoids due to straining. *While sitting on the toilet,* instead of giving way to the self-defeating urge to strain, try a few breathing exercises. Sit up straight, with feet preferably resting on a stool. Slowly inhale while gradually bending forward until your abdomen rests against your thighs. Remain in that position, breath held for five seconds, and then slowly exhale while returning to the original position. Repeat this exercise a few more times. This should stimulate the defecation response such that a movement will begin during one of the exhalations. When the movement begins, continue exhaling in synchronization with the flow of the feces. Once you have developed an integrated bodily response,

you will be rewarded with more positive toilet experiences than you have ever had. Your movements will be full, smooth, continuous releases that leave you feeling light and extremely peaceful. Combining the breathing, defecation reflex, and exercises in this way will lead you to a deeper self-consciousness and body awareness that will extend much farther than its initial goals. Try it and see.

5

Toilet Positions and Activities for Making Elimination Easy and Rewarding

Positions

Primitive man moved his bowels while squatting with his stomach pushed up against his thighs. There are still many toilets in Europe which are simple holes in the cement floor, with fitted platforms on either side for the feet. We were in Japan in 1964 at the time the government began its campaign to install a Western-style seat toilet. The common man resisted and the subsequent compromise was a modernized hole in the floor with a sanitary Western-style flush. I understand that the necessities of modernization have now caused many Japanese to change over to the toilet-seat system, and we are deeply saddened that one more society's peace of bowels will be going down the drain.

The earliest known toilet seat was the Roman latrine at Housteads, the fort on the Roman wall in Northumberland.[1] This was a continuous wooden bench into which holes were carved over a deeply cut sewer. These stalwart legionnaires would sit twenty at a time along the bench, chatting comfortably of their conquests over the Celts and intermittently relieving their bowels into a sewer hundreds of feet below. Let us heartily applaud these warriors for the classical model of the relaxed and thorough movement.

Alas, we in the modern, civilized West rush to and from the toilet without so much as a blink of an eye, and in some cases without so much as a blink of what we thought we were about to do. The original intention of the raised toilet seat was to make the process comfortable enough to entice us into lingering a while. This single virtue is entirely subverted when we move our unenthusiastic bowels on the run. And once subverted, the justification for the seat becomes null and void when we see that its very structure is alien to its purpose. The seat is too high for most of us. In the primitive squatting position, the pressure of the thigh against the belly supports and absorbs the abdominal strain of defecation.

This is presumably why there is such low incidence of hemorrhoids and varicose veins among "squatters" in Africa and Asia.[2] Our Western seat is so high as to remove from our abdomen any support that our legs and thighs might otherwise offer. In fact, those of us with legs shorter than average might even find toes dangling to the floor. Further complicating the issue is the unusual shape of the seat itself, varying from concave to convex, with more thought going to visual charm and appeal than to physical dynamics and functionality. The result is both impaired blood circulation in the region that most needs free circulation, and more important, often an excessively tight juncture of the sphincter muscles at the anus. When, in the difficult period of toilet training our child, he resists the potty with all his might, we should stop for a moment, forget all we've read about the intricacies of his anal stage and rebellion, and consider the ridiculous possibility that he might be trying to tell us something about the self-defeating nature of the system with which we are presenting him.

Obviously, a great deal more evidence is required before the Western world is going to consider the toilet seat to possess a flaw. Moreover, even were it conclusively proved that crouching is better than sitting, it is unrealistic to assume that any changes would be made in the millions of existing seats beyond the legislated warning branded into the rear of the seat, *This seat may be injurious to your health."* The threat of cancer has not caused a significant dent in the smoker population, and we shall similarly assume a lack of concern for the "danger" of hemorrhoids and constipation associated with our toilet seats.

You are now asking, "What are we to do about this—all go out and dig holes in our city parks? Move to the African bush?" I'm afraid this is simply going to be one of those imperfect adaptations to civilized mass-produced absurdity. We shall present a series of imperfect options and you may use your own judgment, try your own experiments. Remember, each individual and his bowel are most unique. Only you, yourself, are the best judge of what works and doesn't for you.

1. To approximate the squatting position more closely, place a stool under your feet as you sit on the toilet seat. The higher the stool, the better. It is no coincidence that the specimen of your feces has been called a "stool" by laboratory technicians. Remember, the ideal position for your thighs should be against your abdomen. The higher the stool, the closer your thighs come to the abdomen. The stool is extremely valuable if you have problems with constipation and/or hemorrhoids. Don't be embarrassed to have your friends and neighbors see a little stool in your bathroom. Be proud that you have the good sense to possess one and use it correctly. After the initial jokes, you may be surprised to find a similar stool in your friend's house the next week.

2. Whether or not you choose to use a stool, it will be of benefit to lean forward slightly on the seat, again with the aim of bringing the abdomen closer to the thighs, and also, this time, relieving some of the pressure against the anus. You may also find that this position is best for reading magazines opened on the floor (which we will cover more extensively in the next section).

3. This is a more radical solution used by some of our younger and more adventurous colleagues. Climb up on the toilet seat and crouch, one foot on either side of the seat. If you are not embarrassed looking at yourself in the bathroom mirror or afraid of heights, this solution seems to duplicate our natural position perfectly. Obviously, you should make sure that both the seat and the entire fixture are securely fastened, or you will suddenly find yourself in the toilet instead of above it.

4. Since we are apparently stuck with this raised system, at least take advantage of its single virtue. Sit there awhile and relax. It is the feeling that we have not enough time that causes us to heave-ho until the only thing on its way out of our anus is this week's new hemorrhoid. There should—must—be time enough for the movement to come of its own accord, without the least bit of straining. Surely you can make time for that. If you are reading this book in the first place, you are concerned enough with your eliminatory system to figure out that coffee break or moment when the kids have gone off to school. We feel that the time spent on the toilet should be one of the most relaxing, meditative points of the day. In the next section, we shall expand on this aspect by discussing various activities that lend themselves to the mood.

Activities

You may remember back to the time you were a child, to the time that those moments on the toilet meant moments of peace, of perfect privacy, with your favorite book, magazine, or comic book, or perhaps just your private thoughts. What has happened to those moments? Chances are that you are too mature, too grownup for such childish pleasures. You have much more important things to do now, like cleaning the house, driving the kids to school, or perhaps breaking in the new secretary or closing that deal. However, if all you can really think about is the dull headache and stuffiness of constipation, along with the excruciating pain of your swollen piles, you may suddenly figure out a way to take a bit more time on the toilet so that you can relax with that book you've been meaning to read.

Once you set your mind to it, you will remember all the things you did as a child to relax on the toilet. In the bathrooms of many homes in America, magazines and open books lie on the radiator cover, the back of the toilet, and even on the floor. It may be a comic book, a *Playboy* magazine, *Newsweek*, *Reader's Digest*, or *War and Peace*. It could be whatever you as an individual find to be most relaxing. Some people keep a pad and a pencil near the toilet and proceed to make lists of things—a task that seems especially suited to relax otherwise emotionally "tight-assed" personalities.

If you are more uninhibited than most of us, or if you live secluded in the wilderness, you might try humming, singing, or even yodeling. You might keep a toy musical instrument such as a little flute or slide whistle next to the toilet to play, or some modeling clay (which by this point you will not be surprised to hear is unconsciously associated with our feces).

Have you ever thought of playing solitaire on the toilet—of course, bending over enough to place cards on the floor, and improving your eliminatory posture at the same time? What about sewing or knitting, especially for those of you who feel too guilty when "wasting time" on such trivial things as a bowel movement? We have had strange reports of a gentleman who had serious difficulties relaxing on the toilet until he began daily to count his money while leaning over the toilet seat. Although at first sight this seems remarkable, we can readily fit this into the behavior of "anal" personalities described in Chapter 2. To the degree that all of us possess such characteristics it would not be a bad idea for each of us to consider the possibility of performing some retentive or "collecting" act while on the toilet, whether it be collecting money, stamps, autographs, paintings, impressive accomplishments, or even aggravations if they do not unrelax us more than they relax us.

All of this is really to say that there is no rule that says we should walk in and out of the toilet tending only directly to the business at hand. It may very well be of benefit for us to deflect our attention, and anxieties, elsewhere—to utilize some of our childhood activities, or to try some new ones. And there is similarly no rule as to which activities will prove most effective for each of us. Enjoy yourself. You may find, as many people have found, that this will prove to be the most rewarding part of your day, one that you look forward to and vigorously defend against all interruptions and aggravations.

It has been suggested to us, however, that excessively long periods of recreational time on the toilet may, in some instances, lead to hemorrhoids. In lengthening your toilet time from but a few minutes to ten or fifteen minutes, we have been trying to reduce the need for impatient straining and to allow for a sense of concentration and calm that will be of value to the proper movement. After that movement comes, you should put your *War and Peace* back upon the shelf and, thus refreshed, go on with your day.

6
Periodic Cleansing Techniques

Enemas

The enema has had a very long history and was known in pre-Christian times.[1] A Roman aristocrat who practiced medicine wrote:

> This remedy should not be tried often, and yet we should not omit to use it once, or at most twice: if the head is heavy; if the eyes are dim; if the disease is in the larger intestine, which the Greeks call the colon; . . . there should then be introduced into the bowel simply water when we are content with a gentle remedy, or hydromel [water and honey] as one a little stronger, or as a soothing enema, a decoction of fenugreek, or pearl barley . . . but a drastic one is sea-water or ordinary water with salt added. . . . . Following upon the injection, the patient ought to keep in bed as long as he can, and not give way to his first desire to defecate; then go to stool only when he must.

The enema (or clyster, as it was first called) continued to be popular throughout the centuries in one form or another. In the seventeenth century, Joseph Lanzoni, a noted Italian physician, explained the proper use of the tobacco smoke enema "when other clysters prove ineffectual, and particularly in the Iliac Passion, and in the Hernia Incarcerata, though it may be used for other purposes, and is peculiarly servicable in an obstinate constipation or obstruction of the bowels."

The smoke was to be introduced to the colon by means of tubing or by the patient's sitting, and stretching his bowels above the fumer. In the eighteenth century, Giuseppi Antonio del Chiappa, another Italian physician, recommended ice-water enemas for treatment of hysteria. As one commentator notes, the icy shock treatment, or rather the anticipation of it, may have done wonders in the *prevention* of hysteria. The clyster gained a unique status when Louis XIV and his entire court became addicted to the use of the enema. The king is reputed to have taken over two hundred enemas in a single year.

We fear however all the groundwork laid by Louis XIV will have been in vain—because at this point in history, there is nothing that creates more terror in the hearts of our children and hospital patients than the whispered "It looks like he's due for an enema." Perhaps it is a violation of all we consider private; perhaps it is the sudden recognition of our vulnerability and the existential terror that goes with it. On the other hand, it may simply be, our fearful expectations of the pain associated with that thick nozzle going up a canal we are convinced is half the size of the nozzle. In any case, we avoid the enema; we do not like even to keep the apparatus in the house, and if we do, we are terribly ashamed of someone else's seeing it there. This is all unfortunate, and we hope that this section may alleviate your fears and misconceptions.

If it is given correctly, as we describe, there is absolutely no reason for the enema to be at all painful. In fact, there are many people who enjoy the process of the treatment even more than the positive effects. Assuming that you are not interested in phenomenologically experimenting with such historical curiosities as ice water, tobacco smoke, or turpentine, you would be hard pressed to find any basis in reality for your fears of excruciating pain.

The enema continues to be an extremely valuable adjunct to bowel care. It is still popular for prevention and cure of colonic disorders, both in our hospitals and in our naturopathic spas and clinics.[2] As we discuss in the next section, the enema is commonly used in fasting procedures, when the waste has no bulk. Because contractile movements of the gut are not stimulated, the waste can remain in the colon for a long time. This causes the reabsorption of the toxic waste into the bloodstream and subsequent headaches associated with the fast.

Enemas are prescribed during a fast as a necessary aid in removal of toxic waste lodged in the convolutions of the colon (and as the consequent cure of the headaches). We have read of no instances in which the enema would not be preferable to "downing" laxatives. The laxative must pass from your mouth through over twenty feet of sensitive passageway before it reaches its final exit. It works as an irritant in causing strong contractile movement of your intestines. There is no reason for you to be so self-destructive as to irritate so much more of your twenty feet of digestive organs than is necessary (assuming that even *any* irritation is necessary!). By using the enema instead, you are limiting your intervention to the last and least vulnerable stages of your system, and are lessening the chances of serious organic damage to your stomach and intestines. Moreover, the effect is felt in but a few minutes. Laxatives have their effects (for better or for worse) in a matter of hours.

Because of their soothing quality, enemas are used before and after operations, and are mandatory *when abdominal pain of any kind* makes use of laxatives downright dangerous. The enema can be used for occasional irregularity, and it can serve you well if taken on trips for the first day's difficulties. The fact that it is recommended over laxatives, however, does not mean that it cannot be overused. It should be an *occasional* aid in getting you over the hump or in periodic cleansing. It is not meant to take the place of all the preventive measures outlined in this book.

Some medical practitioners warn against the dangers associated with too frequent use of the enema—namely, that the abdominal muscles lose their tone and grow lax. This in turn makes it even more difficult to achieve a "regular movement" without resort to external aids which will undoubtedly be even more enemas. You are now back into the addictive cycle that we have continually warned you against. If you are confused and find yourself dashing off a letter to us demanding to know just how often is *too* often, then you have not yet begun to think in the ways that we advocate. The enema is a valuable tool, safer than laxatives, but in no way should it be seen as an excuse for not developing more organic measures and attitudes such as proper diet and exercise. A tool is used "too much" when one *must* use it rather than *wish* to use it. You should not become dependent on *any* bowel aids. Louis XIV did history a service by popularizing the enema. He did history a disservice by his dependency on the enema to the point of absurdity. A practical explanation of the most valuable ways in which to use the enema is included in Appendix B. We wish you a thorough and joyous housecleaning, and now we go on to the second important cleansing modality.

Fasting

For thousands of years fasting has been part of religious ritual. Early Christians fasted two days a week—Wednesday and Friday. Throughout the Orient, fasts have been part of initiation rites. Jesus, Moses, and Elijah all experienced forty-day fasts, and Mohammed, Buddha, and Confucius as well as countless other sages had religious experiences during the course of fasting. It has been commonly held that fasting reduces man's connection to the earthly, trivial pursuits and directs his energies toward higher, spiritual strivings.

Man has also used the fast in the treatment of a number of physical as well as psychological disorders. Most of you have had the terribly frustrating experience of trying to get your sick dog or cat to eat just a little something to "keep up its strength." It is difficult for us to accept the notion that our pets know how to heal themselves better than we do but maybe we can learn something from them. When they are sick or suffering from diarrhea, they try to vomit and then fast for at least a day, thereby ridding themselves of metabolic toxins. Throughout medical history, healers have advised that rest and abstention from food is the best "medicine" for all kinds of sickness.

Naturopaths and folk healers are still advocating the use of the fast. They claim that the fast empties the colon of past wastes, restores tone to the abdominal muscles, and gives the entire digestive system a well-needed rest.[3] Various writers have pointed out that it is no coincidence that so many religious holidays incorporating fasting into their spiritual rituals occur during periods of seasonal change that call for adaptive metabolic changes in our bodies.

Naturopathic practitioners of the fast stress that waste products and their effects lead to various diseases. Ragner Berg, European food expert, has noted that high amounts of protein, beyond the body's needs, leave uric acid crystals in certain body tissue. These crystals, which sometimes resemble fine bits of broken glass, can lodge in connective tissues of the lower extremities causing gout. Many naturopaths think that all the drugs that we have taken at one time or another leave tiny residues that are stored for prolonged periods of time in connective tissue. Because of the self-defeating dietary and bowel habits of modern man, our eliminatory system does not pass wastes from our bodies very effectively.

Why do naturopaths think that the fast can cure these disorders? When the intake of food is stopped, the body immediately uses or oxidizes the available reserves. Whatever is *least* essential to the body is used first—mucus, fat, diseased cells or tissues. Hippocrates said, "If a sick person is fed, one feeds the disease. On the other hand, if the sufferer is withheld from food, the disease is fasted out." The blood and lymph streams use the kidneys, bowels, and skin as exits for the dissolved waste particles. This is why the faster's breath and body odor will increase as the toxins leave the body. It is also the reason that after a fast of from two to three weeks, large stools may still be passed.

In recent years, there has been an increase in the use of fasting therapy by medical practitioners in the U.S. and the Soviet Union. In the U.S., fasting has become an efficient way of achieving major weight loss in extremely obese persons.[4] From the early 1960's until the present time, investigators examined various clinical aspects of long-term fasting. In the last five years, investigators added a protein supplement to the fasts, which were then called "modified fasts." The complaints most commonly reported were intolerance to cold and the embarrassment of halitosis, with a few patients also complaining of dry skin and brittle nails. Euphoria was often reported as weight loss progressed, and improvement was noted in all cases of hypertension. This corroborates the reports from fasters throughout the world that after the first few days of the fast, *there is an uplift of mood and overall feeling of calm and euphoria.*

The following is a description of a more traditional European fasting treatment:[5]

1. Smoking is prohibited during the fast. On an "empty stomach" the effects of all drugs, including tobacco, are exaggerated and therefore counterproductive to the pure, cleansing effect of the fast.

2. An enema is given each morning of the fast, but *no laxatives.*

3. Every morning, the patient receives a fifteen-minute bath in water at body temperature, and then a total body massage.

4. The bath and massage are followed by morning tea and a half hour in bed. Most fasters are tempted to spend the entire day in bed in an enervated half-sleep. In this treatment, the patient is encouraged to get out of bed and go for a nice long walk of up to three hours, after which time he occupies himself *not with sleeping,* but with reading, games, or work therapy. It is certainly true that activity encourages a positive frame of mind and that, most important, exercise of any kind increases the circulation and consequent elimination of waste products from the body.

5. Throughout the day and especially during the daily walks, patients are encouraged to do deep-breathing exercises. Such exercises lead to uplift of mood as well as greater cleansing of the lungs.

6. Breaking the fast with the restitution diet (after twenty to thirty days) is done in an extremely careful way. It begins with a small glass of fruit juice diluted with an equal amount of water. Small glasses of this juice are given at regular intervals throughout the day. On the second day, applesauce, oranges, and other fruits are given along with the juices. On the third day carrots and kefir (or yogurt) are added, from the fifth day on dark rye bread is added, and from the seventh day the patient may eat meat with potatoes, beets, or cabbage, boiled without salt. Fruits and vegetables are given in maximum quantities, and on the eleventh day nuts and cheeses are added. The restitution diet is under the strict control of the clinicians, who are well aware of the potential hazard if the patient, under the increased euphoria and self-confidence, overeats and develops diarrhea and abdominal pain.

The patient's response to this form of treatment is strikingly similar to the statements made in historical sources. During the first few days of the fast, the patient is irritated by all references to food. Perception of food-related stimuli causes a flow of saliva and abdominal pain. Patients sleep poorly, are irritable, and whatever symptoms of sickness were shown before the fast are visibly worse during these first few days. Between the third and fifth day of the fast, hunger pains diminish and may even entirely disappear. Sometimes, patients complain about headaches, vertigo, nausea, and weakness. After twelve to fourteen days, a great change occurs in the state of mind of the patient, called the "acidotic crisis." This point is similar to the fasting crisis reported by other European naturopaths, and to some of the painful visions so poetically reported by religious mystics. In a sense, it is a kind of "wrestling with the devil," or with the "devilish" toxins within one that are finally released from the body. After this crisis, the faster usually experiences great improvement of mood, and feels strong and motivated. It is at this point that the fast is broken and the restitution diet begun. An enema on the second day of the diet usually causes a thorough, cleansing bowel movement, after which the patient's mood becomes euphoric.

After covering the literature on the history of fasting cures, as well as extensively practicing various fasting modalities upon ourselves, we have every reason to believe that a fast of but a few days can have only a positive effect on complaints of constipation, diarrhea, flatulence, and hemorrhoids. Since most readers of this book have been raised in the Western system of overeating, and have been overworking their digestive systems for a number of years, it is hard for us to believe that there is any reader who would not benefit from a short fast. We wish to caution you, however, if you have any hint of a more serious organic disorder, such as those discussed in Chapter 11, that you consult with your doctor before undergoing a fast of longer duration.

There are many approaches to the fast, but there is general agreement on several points:

1. Some liquid must be taken throughout the duration of the fast. You should decide ahead of time whether you wish to drink water, herbal teas with lemon and honey, or fruit or vegetable juices. If you have not fasted before, you should understand that

although a fruit-juice fast may make you feel more emotionally comfortable at first, the acid secretions in your stomach caused by the juice will cause prolonged sensations of hunger, well past the time you would have ceased your fantasies of food if you had been drinking only water or tea. If you choose to take teas, some of the "cleansing" herbs recommended are fenugreek, golden seal, and licorice root. The "calming teas" recommended are valerian, chamomile, and comfrey. A cup of warm tea, with half a teaspoon of honey and lemon juice, should be *sipped slowly* every few hours.

2. Although there are reports of successful thirty and forty-day fasts, there are also reports of hazardous fasts of that length.[6] Someone who has not fasted previously should begin with a short fast of just a few days. A month or so later, a fast of up to a week may be tried. Under no circumstances should a fast of longer duration be attempted without consultation with your doctor. Remember, as in the case of the enema, all potentially good things may be overdone.

3. The preparation for the fast is important. You should plan to fast at a time and place that is comfortable, unpressured, and in fact supportive of your goals. A vacation period, with your family or good friends in sympathy with your fast, is best. A few days before the fast, you should cut out all "concentrated foods" such as meats, cheeses, sugars, etc., and should increase the amount of fruits and vegetables in your diet.

4. During the first few days of fasting, until the wastes which have begun to be released into the circulation are eliminated, you will probably be feeling weak and unable to participate in your normal routine. It is entirely within reason, however, that after elimination on the third day you will feel a great sense of exhilaration and energy. This may turn into a feeling of lassitude or even anxiety within twenty four hours, due to the course of further wastes through the bloodstream before the next elimination. It is most likely that throughout the fast your sense of your body as well as your emotional state will be highly erratic and

most unpredictable, determined as it were by the uncontrollable course of the cleansing. You should remember at all times, however, that the ultimate process is cleansing and constructive, and at those moments of physical discomfort or emotional anxiety, simply know that it is all part of the process of growth toward health and well-being.

5. Sensations of hunger are *worst* the first day of the fast. You are having withdrawal symptoms, not unlike those first days without a cigarette. If you make it past the first day, sensations of hunger will decrease.

6. Some practitioners and clinics recommend laxatives during the fast periodically to relieve the body of wastes, thereby making the fast more comfortable and controllable. On the other hand, there appears to be no necessity for laxatives, and, moreover, the enema, which is more often recommended, has proved more effective and less potentially harmful. You should have moved your bowels by the third day of the fast. If you have not, and are feeling uncomfortable, tense, headachey, or excessively weak, most practitioners would recommend a mild enema. Any of the recipes in Appendix B will be of value, in the evening before going to sleep. As a last resort, and *only* as a last resort, if you simply feel you must take a laxative, Swiss Kriss is a relatively harmless *herbal* laxative, when taken *as directed* with a cup of warm tea before going to bed.

7. Most practitioners feel that breaking the fast is the most important part of the entire fast, one that can either strengthen the gains made during the fast or undo them entirely. After any fast that extends beyond three days, stomach acidity is retarded, the production of hormones and digestive ferments in the pancreas is reduced, and the small and large intestines are reduced in size. Depending on the individual, several days may be required for the reactivation of all organs needed for food assimilation. This means that *you should not resume your normal diet suddenly.* The fast should be broken carefully, either at a predetermined time, or if and when you feel you wish to stop.

Most fasters end their fasts on fruit juice. One glass of juice every hour and a half should bring about a most thorough elimination of all the wastes presently released in your system. In fact, if you have any history whatsoever of a heart condition (in which case, of course, you have consulted with your doctor before attempting the fast) we would recommend that you break your fast with a less radical course of glasses of vegetable juice. Your first bowel movement from the fruit juice should be very loose, watery diarrhea with foamy mucus floating on top. Following this movement, you should rest your system for the remainder of the day, reducing your intake of juice by half.

The second day you may start with fruit juice or whole fruit for breakfast. For lunch and dinner, you may add a raw vegetable salad, and on the third day, cooked vegetables and soured-milk products. The fourth day you may add starches like boiled potatoes and cooked grains, and on the fifth day return to your usual diet. We cannot stress too much the importance of breaking the fast gradually. Your system has been relaxing. To insult it suddenly with a surplus of concentrated food like cheese, eggs, meat, and sugars will cause tremendous pain of indigestion and possibly more serious disorders. If you can maintain the mutually beneficial relationship between your mind and your body for just a few days past the fast, you will be rewarded with sustained calm, balance, and well-being, as well as with a wonderful sense of lightness in body and mind. And your eliminatory system will never have been as good. Within but a few days after the fast your movements will be effortless, smooth, full, and unbroken. A colon which has been rested and cleansed will respond with an elimination more thorough than ever before, and you will be amazed at the sense of lightness and energy that follows every stool.

A great deal more medical research must be carried out on the effects of the controlled fast on all aspects of our minds and bodies. We repeat our first caution, that no one with organic disease, especially disorders of the heart, should undertake a fast of more than a few days. Given this qualification, we are nevertheless tremendously impressed with the results of even a three- to five-day fast both on the elimination system and on the mind. An integral part of the most important religious rituals, the fast is as old as humanity itself. At this point in history, so very many people are driven to overeat out of anxiety and boredom that we might more properly call bowel disorders the "diseases of affluence." In this context, the fast may come to be the most valuable healing mechanism. Not only can it rest and rejuvenate our overworked systems, but it can offer us all a chance to return to ourselves in the midst of our complex industrial society.

PART 3

Bowel Disorders and Their Treatments

7

CONSTIPATION

Most of its ill-effects are caused by its treatment.

—Editorial, **The Lancet**
May 12, 1962

Regular Constipation

Constipation is one of the most common ailments of modern times.[1]
Nevertheless, many people do not even realize that they suffer from it.
There is no general rule for the frequency of bowel movements. As we
said before, a movement once a day may be normal for one individual
and a movement three times a day may be normal for another. The best
frequency for each individual can be gauged only by his general well-
being. If you suffer from dull headaches, feelings of tension and irrita-
bility, flatulence and abdominal distention, colicky pains, belching,
malaise, weakness, and faintness, you may be a victim of irregular or
unsatisfactory movements. A number of years back there was a TV
advertisement for a brand-name laxative. A constipated man went
through his day at work answering all the "how are you's" by "I don't
know, I feel kind of blah." In many real-life instances the symptoms of
constipation are similarly difficult to pin down. There is rarely a sharp
or localized pain. In fact, the sufferer may think he is "under the
weather" or "a bit uptight" or that he "got up on the wrong side of the
bed." These are all nebulous descriptions gaining such remarks as "Get
some sleep," "Take a vacation," and "Have another hamburger, it's
good for you." In fact, too-frequent mention of such ambiguous ailments brings one the appellation of "hypochondriac" or "kvetch." It's a

69

good bet, however, that no one individual is really functioning with optimal health, and that you can certainly benefit from a more effective approach. Those of you who have more serious "blahs" may find that when you improve the regularity and effectiveness of your bowel movements, you will end the complaint that others have told you was "psychological."

What do we mean by regularity? First of all, it is generally agreed that movements which come at the same time every day are more effective than movements that come at unpredictable, irregular times. The most beneficial time of day for elimination is the early morning, before or soon after breakfast. This cleans the intestinal system of waste from the previous day and allows you to begin the new day refreshed. When you begin to move your bowels regularly at the beginning of each day, you will notice the difference. A similar experience occurs when you finally put down a heavy object you have been carrying—the result is a feeling of lightness, except that it is an internal feeling, radiating outward. Your step will be lighter, your posture straighter, your mind and body both more forward and upward thrusting.

There are those who move their bowels two and sometimes three times a day. If these movements are full, effective, and cleansing, then there is nothing abnormal about this, especially if one eats a lot of fibrous foods such as vegetables, fruits, whole grains, which give a greater bulk in the intestinal tract. But if these frequent movements are not effective, they can also be indicative of ailment. If the movements are lumpy, knotted, or excessively fragmented, it may mean that you are ineffectively and incompletely emptying your colon at each sitting. You are apt to cause too great a strain on the abdominal and sphincter muscles, and you may even bring on hemorrhoids, especially if the movements are excessively dry and lumpy.

Let us at this point characterize an "effective" movement. The "regular" movement has to do with the timing and the daily rhythm. The "effective" movement has to do with the nature of the feces itself. As we have detailed in a previous chapter, the color of the feces will vary with the particular foods eaten the previous day. But regardless of the foods eaten, at your optimal level of health, the feces should emerge in a continuous and smooth bolus. One Indian folk healer characterized the perfect bolus as having a texture of fine velour or velvet.

The thickness of the bolus will vary from movement to movement, but generally, the thicker the bolus, the more complete and satisfying it will be. A diameter of about ¾ inch at least is to be desired.

As you maintain a cleansing diet such as is outlined in this book, and the colon begins to wash itself, you should notice that your bolus becomes thicker and as you allow for more roughage to stimulate peristalsis, you should notice that the texture becomes smoother and smoother. Moreover, as your muscles relax through the exercises given in Chapter 4 and 5, your bolus should grow more and more continuous, with fewer knots and other signs of fragmentation.

Generally the feces are a mixture of solid waste and liquid, in varying quantities, so that diarrhea appears as predominantly liquid, and the feces eliminated so sporadically in constipation appear as very dry. The fluid portion of the feces contains such things as phenol (carbolic acid), skatol, indol, bacterial wastes, and even sulfuric acid. In constipation, or a slowing down of elimination, with the wastes remaining longer in the colon, much of this moisture, with its poisons, reenters the blood and lymph, and is subsequently distributed throughout the body, causing many of the ailments associated with constipation. A thick, smooth-flowing bolus is the sign that there is a full and effective evacuation of poisonous wastes. You may begin to notice, for example, that a headache will disappear with the first effective elimination after constipation.

Now let's look at some of the causes of constipation and how to identify them. Let's also talk about ways to prevent constipation or to cure if after it has begun. Our discussion will be brief, serving only to underline the points made in Part II. The factors commonly associated with constipation are: too little liquid, too little bulk in the solid foods, too little physical exercise, too much emotional tension, and mechanical problems (weak muscle tone and obstructive problems).

Water is extremely important to the body for every aspect of the removal of waste. At least one to two quarts a day should be taken in the form of water, herbal teas, and fruit or vegetable juices. Those people who eat large portions of fresh fruit and vegetables each day (foods with a high liquid content) may not require as much liquid, but most people on an average diet do indeed require more than one quart a day of liquids. A deficiency of liquid in the diet may cause irregularity of bowel rhythm as well as dry and hard movements which result in muscular irritation and hemorrhoids. Drinking liquids has a cleansing action like that of water flushing through a pipe, and most practitioners consider internal cleansing as important as the usual external bath or shower.

Roughage is the fiber, the connective tissue in plants. When you put a carrot in a juicer, the pulp remaining after the juice is extracted is fiber. The body acts like the juicer, processing fruit, vegetables, and grains to extract valuable vitamins and minerals in the liquid solution, and pushing the fibrous waste down through the colon. It was once thought that we could extract the vitamins and minerals from these foods mechanically, and simply drink them, avoiding completely the fibrous waste. We have now learned that the fiber, the roughage, is as important to proper digestion and elimination as the vitamins and minerals are to building strong blood and muscles. One Chinese healer offered an intriguing metaphor for the value of fiber. If you have a long pipe that sends water from a well to the kitchen, it periodically becomes internally encrusted with certain forms of dirt. The water sporadically running through the pipe itself is not always sufficient to keep it clean. Periodically a man is called to reach through the pipe with a rough sponge on the end of a long stick, to rub the sides of the pipe clean. This sponge, it was said, is like plant fiber. As we digest fruit, vegetables, and whole grains, the pulp is pushed and squeezed inch by inch along the colon in order to extract its vitamins. In this pushing and squeezing, the fiber brushes against the sides of the colon cleansing away past waste that is beginning to adhere to the internal surface. However, because of its water absorption, it is not so rough as to injure the delicate membranes of the lining. Besides cleansing the membrane, the pulpy nature of the fiber adds a malleable quality to the bolus of the waste forming in the lower colon on its way to the anus, so that it ensures continuity and thoroughness of elimination of all waste in the lower intestines. Some of the healthiest people in the world, people whose elimination is regular and effective, eat primarily fruit, and vegetables, and whole grains (with the bran intact). Any form of whole grain can be beneficial. Westerners can more easily find wheat bran in the form of breakfast cereal, but equally beneficial are such things as rice bran, whole rye, whole millet. When one sees, touches, tastes, the breads of East Europe, Asia, and the Middle East, one wonders how we in America ever came to the form of our present commercial loaves of bread.

As David Ehrlich reported, "After observing the vigorous action my teeth were taking on a Moroccan bread, a friend in Tangiers made a gesture to represent the American bread he had once eaten. That gesture seems to best summarize the state of affairs. He brought his hands apart, creating in the space before him a loaf of American bread. He then brought his hands together as if he were closing the bellows of an accordion—only his hands kept coming together more and more until they rested but two inches apart. And as he laughed, my mind drifted back to a childhood of white bread, like cotton candy—of how I would use it for fishing bait—wetting a whole piece of bread, squeezing it until it was molded into a doughy blob about three-quarters of an inch in diameter." A nation depending on roughage like this would not have an easy time at elimination. So add whole grains to your diet. Buy breads that don't close like accordions, but breads that will offer resistance to the movements of your colon. We include in Appendices A, C, and E a list of recipes for combinations of these fibrous foods, popular around the world.

Sometimes, neurological disorders, multiple pregnancy, or a life without physical exercise of any sort causes a lack of control of abdominal muscles, and there is not enough muscular stimulation of peristalsis or the defecation reflex. In Chapter 4 and Appendix D we give you many exercises especially used to contract and expand the intestinal cavity, to aid in alleviating constipation. We must expect that the thoroughness and vigor of our internal muscular movements such as peristalsis will be only as active as our external muscles.

Anxiety and emotional tension cause a corresponding physical tension in the internal organs. Peristalsis is inhibited from proper rhythmic movement. The defecation reflex is inhibited, and the sphincter muscles are too tight to allow proper elimination. And regardless of how much liquid or roughage is taken in, digestion is impaired, and gas and constipation result. One article in a British medical journal characterized sufferers of constipation as individuals who are "fence-sitters" when it comes to making decisions.[2] There seems a cyclical interaction between mind and body that was discussed more thoroughly in Chapter 2, but at this point let us simply say that all the factors associated with constipation are interrelated, and a complete and satisfactory prevention of constipation must entail dealing with all these factors together.

Constipation which does not yield to natural treatment should always be thoroughly investigated by your doctor to make sure there is no mechanical obstruction, such as a tumor. And under no circumstances can we sanction the abuse of laxatives. The medical profession as well as many folk healers are adamant about the dangers of such abuse. Poor muscular tone and faulty peristaltic movements can result from continued overstimulation by laxatives. Recent articles in leading medical journals note that most of constipation's ill effects are caused by its treatment. Researchers cite the dangers of laxative abuse as ranging from simple worsening of bad habits to depletion of body potassium, weakening of intestinal motility, and severe kidney damage.[3]

The "irritant" laxatives such as castor oil, croton oil, and most mineral oils cause loss of important vitamins and minerals as well as weakness of intestinal motility.[4] Continued use of mineral oil has resulted not only in reduced intestinal motility but also, in some cases, in cancer of the colon and bowel. A single laxative drug, sold as Senokot in pharmacies, is prescribed *for limited use.* Senna is an anthracine drug that stimulates the nerves that increase peristaltic movements. It will irritate these membranes when its use is prolonged and progressively escalated. Senokot is only to be used in the most stubborn cases of constipation.

Our general rule for treatment is as follows: if you feel you are constipated, try the natural laxative foods, fluids, and exercises which we describe in Part II and the Appendices. If you don't see a clear improvement over the next week, and total cure within a few weeks, see your doctor. He may then prescribe Senokot or some other treatment. *Do not use any over-the-counter laxative without the approval of a doctor.*

Regular and perfectly effective movements will not happen over-night. Adding more liquid and roughage to your diet and exercising more will slowly begin to change the pattern of elimination. This in turn may give enough positive reinforcement to your taking control of your own life so that you become less tense. Merely reading this book may build your confidence in your power to improve your health and regularity. As a result, you may begin to notice a change in your movements even before you have begun to change your eating and exercising habits. The interrelationship between mind and body is a complex one, varying from one individual to another. We advise equal concern with all four of the factors (liquid, diet, exercises, emotional equilibrium) to ensure the most rapid and secure improvement of your health. (See the folk cures presented in Appendix C, the exercises listed in Appendix D, and the home laxative preparations included in Appendix E.)

Traveler's Bowels

While hard at work on the chapter on diarrhea, David Ehrlich received word that two of his films were to be shown at a European film festival. What follows is his personal account of his trip to the festival.

I packed my bags, and I was off to Poland and France, suddenly oblivious to my previous concerns with feces and colons. The fates must have been dogging my tracks in laughter, however, because my attentions very quickly turned back to the subject of the present book. I was to be forced to spend six weeks phenomenologically dealing with what I shall forevermore call "traveler's bowels." In other words, I became irregular.

One comes to expect a bit of traveler's *diarrhea* when traveling below the equator. When traveling to Europe, however, one securely throws away sulfa drugs and iodine tablets, and even freely drinks the tap water, because "one just does not develop diarrhea in Europe." What I had forgotten from my past trips, however, and what is rarely reported in medical research, is that equally difficult problem suffered by great numbers of travelers in *all* parts of the globe—constipation, with its accompanying aggravations such as headaches, feelings of weakness, bloatedness, and in some cases the resurgence of hemorrhoids. Now, if you've carefully read the earlier part of this chapter on constipation, you may already be thinking of why travel would leave one prey to such a thing. To tell the truth, when I left on my trip, I was rather looking forward to a bit of relief from writing this book and was quite dismayed to find myself living an entirely new chapter.

After ten hours of an Icelandic Airlines flight and a fifteen-hour train trip from Luxembourg to Vienna, followed by an overnight train from Vienna to Cracow, Poland, not to mention the next two days sitting in a movie theater in Cracow, I was entirely and unrelentingly constipated. I was weak, generally irritated at the most trivial things, and to make the condition sound thoroughly textbookish, I had a dull headache. Worst of all, however, I felt the deep sense of hypocrisy of the constipated expert on bowels. All right, I thought, the only right thing for me to do was to put my bowels where my typewriter was, and in so doing maybe learn a few more things in the process. Aha, I thought, what better way to illustrate what I'd been talking about than a personal case history. Rather than resort to a laxative, so ubiquitously displayed in the little drugstores, I would analyze the causes of my irregularity step by step for myself as well as for the readers of this book, and then, acting on this knowledge, would self-help away the constipation.

First, I realized that I had been sitting for three days. Playing out the role of big-shot filmmaker, I had been taking taxis in Vienna and then Cracow instead of my usual walking explorations. My sphincter muscles had been chronically tightened together in this sitting position, and with so little exercise, my abdominal muscles had temporarily lost their flexibility and tone. Well, at a film festival, I could hardly avoid sitting in the theater for the rest of the week, but I began walking to the theater, taking circuitous routes. Once I began doing this, I reexperienced the joys of walking in a foreign country, the feelings of independence, of exhilaration, of the capacity to take in everything and everyone around me, and the ease with which one can meet people, on the street, in stores, in parks. I began to feel better physically. The headaches disappeared, but, I'm sorry to say, by the end of my fourth day out of the U.S. I had only moderate success on the toilet.

I next addressed myself to my diet. I would have liked to have gotten some nice ripe fruit and some raw vegetables. I would have been ever so pleased to enter a Polish restaurant and order a plate of whole rice or rye. I was, however, in Cracow. I could order pork sausage, lamb, beef, potatoes, and bread, but it would be a rare chef who would fix up a vegetable salad, whole-grain dish, or the like. I had heard that Polish yogurt was delicious, but I hadn't seen a single container of it in three days in Cracow. As for fruit, at a market the day before I had caught a glimpse of a tiny basket of shriveled apples. I grew noticeably depressed. I could certainly institute healthful control of my physical actions to the extent of walking more, but how on earth could I maintain control of my diet in the face of such contrary realities?

As it turned out, the answer was simply to try harder. Upon inquiry, one storekeeper who spoke German told me that I could buy yogurt at his store or at one of a multitude of others, but that I would have to get to the store by nine in the morning at the latest. It seems that the government-owned distributor delivers a few yogurts to each of the appropriate stores and that these yogurts are sold out very quickly to the elderly people who shop early in the morning. Well, this was fine with me. It would add rather nicely to my early-morning jaunts along the streets.

Fresh fruits and vegetables were still a problem. In America we are used to all sorts of fruits and vegetables at our neighborhood supermarket. Most of these are imported from other parts of America or even from different parts of the world. In a country like Poland, where the borders are not so freely opened and where the country itself does not embrace as large a climate area as does the U.S. one gets only that produce that is in season in the particular area, and not very much of it. Well, I did find a larger open-air market on the other side of the city where I could get fresh apples as well as raw whole buckwheat. I didn't find bounteous vegetable stands, but in many of the small neighborhood stores I found jars of delicious pickled vegetables: sauerkraut, red cabbage, pickled beets, pickles. Mixed with yogurt, these lactic-acid products made wonderful lunches and snacks. So there I was, finally exercising and eating intelligently, if a bit uninterestingly, but still no great success on the toilet. I couldn't imagine what else I could do, and wondered how long the author of a book on bowels could survive constipation—and what cause of death would be printed on the book jacket. After all, this was now the fourth straight day! I was continually promising myself that I would not, *in any circumstances,* take a laxative, no matter how herbal it was touted to be. It was most difficult, however, to walk past those little Polish drugstores with those enchanting laxative displays in the window. I felt like the person who is trying to give up smoking, valiantly passing the tobacco store.

It was not before the last day of the festival, my fifth day in Europe, that the awakening and subsequent release came. A Polish friend said to me, "Well, David, I bet you'll be glad to take a week's relaxation between festivals. I know you've been up tight here." An hour later I was walking back to the hotel feeling more relaxed, thinking of what my friend had said. Yes, of course I would be glad to relax. I was never more "uptight." This had been my first festival. I was extremely nervous, controlled, afraid to *let go* in every sense of the word, especially the sense most relevant to this book. I had been so controlled that the tightening of my sphincter muscles from all the initial sitting had been continued even through the subsequent walking. There had been an emotional, psychological constipation, an uptightness that would have persisted despite the external health measures such as exercise and diet. Just the consciousness, the sudden awareness of the relationship between my mind and my body, made me feel more relaxed, more in control of my destiny so that I *could* relax my self-defeating control of my muscles.

That night I boarded a train back to Vienna. I noticed that the particular car was completely empty. Within an hour I answered nature's call, and let me tell you, ladies and gentlemen, a full and thorough movement after five days of constipation is all but made in heaven. It was when I sat there luxuriating on a toilet in an empty car that it occurred to me how important, how absolutely necessary it was to a proper bowel movement that one feels secure in his position—that one not feel pressured by a knock or a call at the door. For the five days in Europe, not once until that very moment could I feel that sense of security. The Icelandic flight had four bathrooms for over three hundred people. (And you know the effect on those three hundred people of soda, coffee, wine, peanuts, dinner, after-dinner liqueur and more coffee.) The train to Vienna had one toilet for a car of over fifty people. The overnight train to Cracow had packed seventy five people into a one-toilet car. Once in Cracow, rather than pay forty dollars a night for a room with toilet, I chose to pay fifteen dollars a night for a room without toilet. This meant a toilet in the hall shared with twenty other people. For Europeans brought up in this system, where all space and privacy are at a premium, adaptations are made at a very young age to a sort of invulnerability of purpose in the public toilet—an invulnerability that is not shaken by the public WC in most European cities in which to use the toilet stall one enters the large room, pays an elderly woman a few cents, is given a foot or so of very rough toilet paper, and is ushered into a stall by the woman who stands closeby outside while you sit nervously upon your throne. (Yes, when you are finished, she will rush in after you to reflush the toilet and clean up for the next person.) We Americans are often prey to what I now call the *"self-concious bowel."* Even some Europeans I have spoken to have irregularity problems in the face of potential privacy invasions. I realized then, and had it confirmed again and again in talks with other travelers, that the self-conscious bowel is our greatest problem while traveling, whether traveling to Poland or even to our aunt's house in the next city. With most forms of self-consciousness, of course, one gains more and more confidence and control the more one goes through the particular experience. After a few weeks in Europe, none but the hopeless remain self-conscious with the woman in the public toilet, and if there is a knock at the door while we are sitting in the train toilet, we have learned to say "Besetz" or "Occupado" with just the right amount of firmness and go on calmly with what we are doing.

For the rest of the five weeks in Europe, I remained almost continually regular. No matter what city I was in, I always found something I could add to my diet to provide appetizing bulk—apples, dried figs, some fresh or soured vegetable, or some raw grain. And I always found some lactic-acid product such as yogurt, kefir, buttermilk, sauerkraut, or even honey. I found that I loved the tastes of the different mineral waters all through Europe. These mineral waters are usually very slightly laxative in their balance and seemed to add just the right touch to my digestive powers while traveling. I spent hours walking through cities, not only for the exercise but because it proved to be the most fun, the most appropriate way of meeting interesting and warm people throughout my travels.

Constipation and indigestion can make even the best planned trip terribly uncomfortable. So many people expressed regret over their overindulgence, choices that were made so impulsively in restaurants and coffeeshops. So many people regretted that they hadn't planned their trips with more space between planes and trains just for relaxing. And so many people were not prepared to cope with the self-conscious bowel. If you are going to so much trouble to plan an itinerary, why not just sit down and take into account some of the possible causes of traveler's bowel and see if you can't prevent it. We offer some simple suggestions. You may feel that some of them are quite obvious; however, it is sometimes the obvious that is overlooked:

1. Before you leave for your trip, have a good bulky meal of fruit, vegetables, and grains.

2. Unless you are absolutely starving, you need not eat all the rich, poorly balanced food that is handed to you on the plane. Remember, you will be expected simply to sit there for a number of hours after eating!

3. Plan on staying in a nice hotel room with toilet on your first day abroad—before boarding the train, bus, or plane to your first destination, even if that first day is spent in a lackluster city.

4. That first day in the city, go for a long *leisurely* walk. Meander over to the open-air market and buy some nice juicy fruit. By the way, you may find, as we do, that these markets are the most lively and interesting attractions of the city.

5. Schedule the next stage of your journey on the second day at the earliest, and schedule it late enough in the day to give yourself enough time for your own rhythm of morning rituals.

6. Think about the self-conscious bowel syndrome *before* you even begin your trip. Go back over in your mind similar experiences in your past. Imagine what it will be like on the trip.

Imagine the most difficult experiences possible. This is called the "work of worrying." Such rehearsals, in moderation, often lessen the later symptoms. Most important, understand that the symptom is quite common and that it disappears with repeated experience. So, don't worry too much!

7. Before you leave, in the absence of impulsive temptations, make a reasonable assessment of your particular digestive capacities and needs, and then try to stick to it in Europe, or wherever you are going.

8. Although most hotels and pensions around the world offer breakfast free with the room, unless you have passed your life happily in breakfasts of coffee and rolls with butter and jam, you would do well to pass them up on your trip. You can purchase some delicious fruit and yogurt the day before or on your early-morning constitutional, and then walk to a beautiful park or lakeside to eat. You might even summon up the courage to bring it right into the breakfast room and set an example for every immobile bowel in the house.

Here is one last thought which very well might take the place of all the above rules: *overindulgence in foods is often a sign that you are underindulging in other aspects of your life.* If you are enjoying the places you are visiting, the people you are meeting, and the self you are experiencing, you will have absolutely no need for the kinds of eating that bring digestive troubles. You will also possess enough self-confidence to get over the self-conscious bowel quickly. So, most important of all, have a truly wonderful trip.

8
Diarrhea

Two thousand years ago, Aretaeus the Cappodocian wrote that diarrhea "consists of the discharge of undigested food in a fluid state."[1] This definition still holds today, as most physicians would agree that diarrhea is the passage of stools containing excess water with increased frequency.

The intestines are normally exposed to huge quantities of liquid every day, not only in the form of our glasses of water, milk, tomato juice, and Coke, but also in the liquid content of our fresh fruits, vegetables, and even bowls of rice or spaghetti. In the overwhelming majority of cases, this liquid is quite simply and effectively absorbed. In some instances, however, something irritates the bowel and causes the peristaltic waves to become fast and violent, thereby pushing all you have eaten and drunk through your intestines at tremendous speed. There is simply no time for the intestines to absorb the quantities of liquid. In fact in some cases additional liquid may be resorbed back into the bowel. There is great pain in the abdomen that begins as recurrent spasms on one side and develops, as inflammation progresses, into constant aching throughout the abdominal region. There may even be vomiting, which means that the stomach is involved as well as the intestines.

In the majority of diarrhea cases, which occur suddenly and startlingly, both medical practitioners and folk healers view the symptom, the violent intestinal spasms, as nature's way of ridding the body of noxious agents. One physician, Dr. E. J. Gangarosa of the Atlanta Center for Disease Control, in an article on the treatment of diarrhea, went so far as to quote the words of the English poet Milton: "Curse not nature, for she hath done her part. Do thou but thine."[2] Dr. Gangarosa states that the antimotility drugs (which decrease the violent abdominal spasms) *may actually do more harm than good, by compromising the diarrhea's organic cleansing of bacterial disease from the bowel.*

Folk healers have often smiled at the complaint of patients that their diarrhea is uncomfortable. These healers say that the discomfort should *not* be used as a motivation for a drug or herb to stop the process of a simple illness. Rather, the discomfort should be used as a poignant future reminder to avoid or moderate whatever food, drink, or activities led to the diarrhea in the first place. Comparisons are drawn to animals in the wild which may eat several kinds of food in a single day and get a stomach upset from one of them. After the course of vomiting and diarrhea, and a bit of fasting, that animal will *never* touch the offending food again. Would that humans were so reasonable!

Beyond the cleansing effects of a temporary case of diarrhea, there are several more serious side effects that may endanger your life if the diarrhea continues for long periods of time. These have to do with the body's continual loss of water through the bowel as well as loss of the electrolytes that pass with it, such as potassium, sodium, chloride, and bicarbonate. When you begin to feel weaker and weaker during the diarrhea bouts, it is because of the loss of the potassium salts as well as because of the acid-alkaline imbalance that results from it. A *severe* and *continuous* bout with a diarrhea-producing illness, such as cholera, may kill a patient in a few days through dehydration (loss of water) and loss of potassium salts. In most cases of diarrhea, therefore, both doctors and folk healers will advise gentle replacement of water and mineral salts.[3] The patient should obviously stop the intake of any solids, for they would further inflame the system as they exit, and they would, in any event, be to no avail. On the other hand, potassium-rich glasses of fruit juice, mixed with a little ordinary table salt (sodium chloride) and a little honey (rich in glucose, which is necessary for absorption of salts), may be slowly sipped. A second glass of water, mixed with a little baking soda (sodium bicarbonate) may be drunk at the same time, especially in the event of nausea and vomiting.[4] (Precise recipes and instructions are given in Appendix F.) In some severe and advanced cases, when the inflammation has already proceeded to the stomach so

that you cannot even swallow liquids without vomiting, a hospital will
be necessary. There you will be given the liquids and salts directly
through a vein. You would be wisest not to let things get to this stage.
This means that at the first sign of diarrhea, slow down your worldly
activities, get plenty of rest, and keep up the replacement of liquids
and salts.

It is now time to look at the various causes of diarrhea.

The Nervous Bowel

This complaint seems to afflict extremely large numbers of people in
our Western societies.[5] The pressures of performance, of measuring up
to other people's expectations of us (as well as to our own) can cause a
little tummy upset, otherwise proverbially known as "the flutters" or
any number of expressions all of which primarily refer to the need
suddenly to "run" to the toilet and relieve the contents of our bowels in
a rush of brown liquid. Such expressions as "shitting in his pants" give
emphasis to the connection between diarrhea and fright-connected
nervousness. All of us can remember back to our childhood when we
had the walk-on in the school play, or that exam we knew we were
going to fail, or that date with our dreamboat. A sudden onset of
diarrhea was really a symbolic inflammation of our self-confidence, a
loss of control and fear for our immediate destiny.

At its extreme, when such diarrhea bouts increase in frequency we
may become extremely withdrawn, afraid to assert ourselves in the
human arena for fear of further debilitating bouts and consequent embarrassment. A chronic condition, alternating with constipation, may
lead to irritable colon syndrome (which we cover in Chapter 11). In
general, though, most cases of nervous bowel are mild, more frequent
in the young and in females, and are related to specific anxiety-
producing events.

What can we do about the nervous bowel? Well, first of all, it often
helps just to realize that it is a common problem, that many people
have it, and that there is a term in common usage that is meant to
describe it. There is no need to be afraid of some unknown physical

illness that you imagine to be even much worse than the nervous or functional symptom. Many people have found relief in the vast number of contemporary relaxation methods. Any or all the exercises we list in Chapter 4 might prove to be of benefit to you in overcoming your nervousness and further taking your mind off "the anxious event." Some people find that anxiety can be worked off through vigorous exercise—competitive sports, simple exercises, or maybe just a nice long walk. Others practice deep-breathing techniques such as yoga. Any number of things that take your mind and anxieties off the fear of performance are likely to be of value, things like reading your favorite novel, playing a musical instrument, even watching the soaps on TV.

If you are naturally introspective, it may be of value to you to address yourself frontally to the seat of your anxieties. Remember back to times you may have been just as anxious as you are now. Remember how you thought the moment would never end. And then think of how you actually felt during or after the event. Chances are, that the anxiety before the event was much more intense than during it. This is because anticipatory fear, or phobic anxiety, refers more to irrational things than to the immediate reality. In the presence of the immediate reality, there is no substantiation for such a high level of anxiety and the anxiety goes away. It may also be good for you to ask yourself the question "What is the very worst that can happen to me should I perform badly?" Really wrack your brain to come up with the worst possible consequence. Make sure, though, that it is a specific and concrete consequence. When you do this, the anxiety may decrease, because *no specific consequence can be quite so painful as the irrational phobic anxiety.*

In any event, you should understand the nervous bowel is directly related to the fear of performance. Use the fact of the diarrhea as grounds for a little self-analysis. Somewhere in your past you have developed insecurities and fears about failing, about rejection. If you focus on the actual fears and try to assess the forthcoming event as concretely as possible, you may very well force your fears into consciousness and out of the realm of your bowels. You will thereby decrease the extent of the fears, render them more susceptible to reason, and be well on your way to curing the nervous bowel.

Psychotherapy is often an invaluable aid to overcoming the physical symptoms, and many psychologists and psychiatrists have reported positive results in treating patients by means of hypnosis.[6] Under hypnosis, patients are told that they can have control over the nerves to the gastrointestinal tract, that they will be able to control peristalsis, and that their bowel habits will return to normal. The patients are then taught self-hypnosis by means of which they are to give themselves similar suggestions. The reported results have been extraordinary, giving great weight to the thesis that man *has* much greater control of his "autonomic" functions than ever before realized.

Dietary Diarrhea

One medical writer reported the case of a sixty-eight-year-old farmer who was referred for investigation of a nine-year-old case of chronic diarrhea. Two days after his admission to the hospital, his diarrhea spontaneously subsided, and he began passing one formed (normal) stool daily. When asked whether his hospital diet was in any way different from his home diet, he replied, "No, except that I'm not having my prunes." It seemed that nine years earlier, a neighbor had lauded prunes as a "healthy" food, and from that time on he had eaten a large bowl of prunes each morning for nine years. In all the nine years, he had not thought it important enough to mention to his doctor, who unwittingly prescribed a number of drugs which had no effect on the diarrhea. Prunes, of course, in moderation are an excellent aid to a constipated bowel, but a large dish of them every morning for nine years might very well cause a bit of diarrhea.[7]

There are many foods that are known to cause diarrhea when *overeaten*. Some people have strong reactions to coffee, for example. Above we gave you the example of prunes, but all sweet fruits, such as figs, apples, pears, etc., may cause diarrhea. In fact, all of those delicious juicy fruits that are given as a preventive and cure for constipation may, on overuse, lead to diarrhea. *All unripe fruits may lead to diarrhea* if even a small amount is eaten. We remember a manual on raising parakeets we pored over thirty years ago. We were told to give our parakeet plenty of raw apples and other fruits in addition to the normal amount of seeds and grains and traditional cuttlebone. In the event that the droppings became too dark and hard, we were to increase the feeding of raw apple, and if the droppings became too soft, to decrease the feeding of fruit.

Our bodies, like that of the parakeet or of any living organism, are held in balance by a multitude of elements. It is up to us as individuals to find the diet and modes of living that contribute to our best balance. Many people in tropical countries can eat over five pounds of fruit daily without problems. There are some people in northern climates, however, who face diarrhea with less than a pound of fruit. If you have increased your intake of fruit through taking Chapter 3 literally and now find that you have merely exchanged constipation for diarrhea, you have obviously overdone things a bit. Eat a few less prunes, figs, and bananas, and continue on with this chapter.

Practitioners now feel that since most of our foods contain additives—about which, to say the least, we are poorly informed—it seems likely that many cases of unexplained diarrhea may be due to additives. To bring the point home clearly, we offer a summary of an excellent recent report from the University of Miami Medical School of a sixty six-year-old woman with a three-month history of chronic incapacitating diarrhea, with as many as *twelve to fifty stools per day!* A complete and expensive series of tests were done with no clear results. Finally, when her dietary history was reexamined, it was found that the patient habitually chewed fifty to a hundred sticks of sugarless chewing gum daily to aid in weight reduction. Upon abrupt withdrawal of chewing gum, all diarrhea ceased.[8] The sugar alcohol sorbitol, used as a sweetener in many dietetic foods, has a mildly laxative effect in doses over 20 grams. It causes water to be drawn osmotically into the colon. Each stick of chewing gum this woman had taken contained 1.7 grams of sorbitol. Chewing fifty to a hundred sticks a day gave her an average of 85–170 grams a day! Even chewing as few as ten sticks a day would have brought her close to the laxative effect (that's about a single pack of gum). Doctors have coined a new phrase for the symptom, *"chewing gum diarrhea."* It is reassuring to know that diagnosticians will now ask diarrhea patients how much dietetic chewing gum they chew. It is more than disconcerting, however, to consider the possibility that in the coming years, thousands of new phrases and diagnostic questions may have to be added to the books, corresponding to the use of the multitude of chemical wonders we daily ingest into our systems. And we will be the guinea pigs who will lend our health to modern medical discoveries of the negative side effects of these additives.[9] It is said that Napoleon lost the Battle of Waterloo because he delayed half a day, giving the enemy time to regroup and unite, and that he delayed because he was suffering from a difficult case of the runs. Let us take heart. Let's ship our tons of dietetic this and that over to the warriors of other lands who may someday face us on the battlefield. Let's deluge them with our goodies that are so brightly wrapped and so entertainingly advertised, and maybe, just maybe, we can win the next war by default!

What can we do about these additives? Well, first of all, if we value the health of our intestinal systems, we'd better start reading the labels. We can find out what the ingredients are, what side effects have been reported, by writing to the Food and Drug Administration in Washington, D.C. We can write those companies that produce foods we find contain harmful or potentially harmful substances without proper warning. Learn how to cook foods that have not been tampered with.

Lactose Intolerance

Deficiency of intestinal lac*tase* is an extremely common trait in adult humans. It occurs in 10 percent of Caucasians and in a much higher percentage of all Oriental and black adults. Lactase is required to break down the sugar, lac*tose,* in milk. When we are deficient in lactase, the lactose ferments in the intestines, causes gas, and eventually acts as an irritant, causing diarrhea.[10] Most people with lactase deficiency have already learned to avoid milk and milk products. Oriental peoples have developed marvelous alternative products, with all the nutrient quality of milk but without the lactose. All are derived from the soy bean; there is soy milk, soy-milk cheese (tofu), and soy-milk custard. If, as a milk drinker, you are subject to bouts of diarrhea, try eliminating milk from your diet for a few weeks and see if the condition clears up. If you find that you do have a lactase deficiency, ask your doctor about the many enzyme tablets on the market that will aid your digestion of milk. Or you might try limiting your milk intake to fermented-milk products such as yogurt and buttermilk, in which the lactose has already been broken down by the fermentative action of the bacteria.

Traveler's Diarrhea

There are several factors involved in traveler's diarrhea.[11] First is the nervous bowel mentioned earlier in this chapter. Any trip is full of anticipatory excitement and anxiety. Will we make the plane on time? Will the plane reach the destination in time for us to catch that train? What is our hotel like? Will the children be all right at home with their grandmother? Did we remember to lock all the doors and windows? There is literally no end to all the things we can find to worry ourselves about if we are so inclined. One psychologist summed up all these specific worries under a single heading—anxiety about the unknown future. We are breaking our daily habits and patterns to venture into uncharted territory, a new place, a new set of activities, of people. As we described in Chapter 7 on traveler's constipation, you might react to the newness and the anxieties by a kind of holding back, a tightness. On the other hand, you might very well "let it all go" in uncontrollable bowels. As you are sitting there on the plane, hurtling to the unknown while downing drinks and foods you never would have touched before if you had had to pay for them, it is anyone's guess as to whether you'll wind up with constipation or diarrhea. Everything we have told you about prevention of traveler's constipation is of value in treating or, hopefully, preventing, traveler's diarrhea. Relax, eat moderately of the food on the plane, drink plenty of liquids, don't rush off for the next leg of your trip, get lots of exercise, and again, just relax.

There is, however, one slight addition to our concerns about traveler's diarrhea that was not of issue in our constipation chapter, and this is the kind of diarrhea that comes from the change of bacteria, whether it be called "Montezuma's Revenge" or the "Tokyo Trots." Everyone builds up a relationship with the varieties of bacteria that are to be found in one's native section of the earth. For hundreds of thousands of years, people's means of travel were relatively slow. They were able to adapt, step by step, to the various bacteria of the lands they traversed. Even then, vast epidemics arose throughout history when cultures would intermix. Nowadays when our little bodies can be in New York one day and then in Mexico City or Bangkok in less than a day, our resistance systems are taken completely by surprise and we find ourselves, after but a single hot tamale or pork kum chow, lying in bed in excruciating pain, weakness, and diarrhea. If we are especially careful, and rich, we may bring with us, our own cook, who prepares foods brought from our hometown grocer, kept uncontaminated in antiseptic vats. Even if we are this rich, however, we might find that such a careful vacation is really not a very joyous one.

Everyone seems to agree that in trips to tropical climates we should drink only bottled water, avoiding the germ-ridden tapwater and iced beverages. A British medical convention in Mexico City found, however, that even those physicians who drank the bottled water, and who avoided the germ-ridden tapwater, came down with diarrhea.[12] The foods that seemed to cause the worst cases were uncooked, raw salads, which offered excellent breeding grounds for tropical bacteria. Most of the medical sources seemed to agree on the following precautionary measures, with no guarantee, however, that they would do any good at all:[13]

1 On arrival at your destination, *don't eat right away.* Get some exercise, *then get some rest, preferably sleep.*

2. On the first day or two, refrain from being a "sport." Tolerate the jokes of friends and loved ones and stick to the bland international menu until your body builds up its resistance gradually. For those same two days, don't drink unboiled water or raw milk, or eat breads, fresh fruit, or vegetables or fish. What *can* you eat? Well, you can eat cooked vegetables, soups, yogurt, or anything bottled. Or you can first thoroughly wash and peel your fruits and vegetables, European style.

3. Before your trip abroad, check to see which diseases are "popular" at your destination. Make sure you have the necessary innoculations.

4. If, like most people, you absolutely ignore such glum precautions on your first great vacation in years, you might bring along some Vioform, a CIBA brand of drug containing iodine. Follow the instructions on the label, *don't* overdose, and check with your doctor first (it should *not* be taken by anyone with thyroid or goiter condition). If you find yourself in deepest Africa or India with only the water in the village well to drink, you might take out your handy-dandy first-aid kit, open the bottle of iodine, put a single drop in a pint of water, wait a half hour, and have a foul-tasting but healthily antiseptic glass of water.

5. If even the Vioform or iodine have been too much effort for you and you find yourself lying there on the bed in pain, interrupted only by the runs to and from the toilet every ten minutes, look on the bright side. Your system is having a much-needed cleansing which, if it doesn't lead to cholera or typhoid, will leave you painfully refreshed in but a couple of days.

Gastroenteritis

"Gastroenteritis" is a general term referring to inflammation of the intestinal tract. Most of us have had it at least once. Maybe you called it a "stomach flu" at the time. If you did, you were falling prey to the American confusion of terms. There is no proven relationship between influenza and gastroenteritis.

The symptoms of gastroenteritis are unmistakable. We come home from the office and are suddenly stricken with vomiting, diarrhea, and abdominal cramps. We grow weaker by the minute as the diarrhea persists. We get headachey, there are pains in our muscles and joints, and along our shoulders and back. For brief moments, we may think we are about to die. But within a surprisingly short time, from one to three days, the illness passes. Scientists are not clear as to the mechanisms of contagion of these minor inflammations. They are less clear about the means to control them. Antibiotics and sulfa drugs are not effective, and the typical race to the aspirin bottle or to the TV-advertized pain-killers containing aspirin, may do more harm than good. As a stomach irritant, aspirin will cause even greater inflammation of the stomach lining.

The treatment of gastroenteritis is simple.[14] Abstention from solid foods and plenty of rest and liquids with salts and a bit of sugar. If the illness is more severe, and inflammation of the stomach makes it very difficult to swallow liquids, then you should very slowly sip a glass of water with baking soda. This will settle your stomach enough so that you can take the other salt-sugar broths or juices. If you notice no relief within thirty-six hours, you'd do best to call your doctor, who will check for more serious illness. You shouldn't take any other drug without checking with your doctor first.

Drug Diarrhea

As we stated in the section on dietary diarrhea, chemicals added to food may cause side effects of diarrhea. In much the same way, chemicals taken not as food additives, but as healing agents, may have similar negative side effects.[15] There are some drugs that, if taken in large doses, will cause diarrhea. There are others, like digitalis (used for heart ailments), that cause diarrhea under prolonged cumulative use. Other people have totally unexpected and individual negative reactions to certain drugs like aspirin. Other drugs, such as a number of those used to counteract the pain of arthritis, cause side effects of gastroenteritis. Practitioners are familiar with negative side effects of certain drugs but unfamiliar with others. If you have an attack of diarrhea that does not clear up, and you have been taking a particular drug for another condition, make sure to ask your doctor for his knowledge of the side effects of the drug. For the most part, as we have repeatedly stated, you should have asked for this information at a much earlier time. If the drug concerned was *not* prescibed by your doctor, withdraw from it immediately and see if the diarrhea stops.

There is a particular form of drug diarrhea that is related to antibiotics. Most antibiotics work by destroying or limiting the number of bacteria that are overpowering the body in various forms of infection. The science is not as precise as it could be, however, and within a few days the bacteria that are normally in balance with the destroyed bacteria, but which are not similarly susceptible to the antibiotic, simply overgrow because they are no longer opposed, causing an enteritis and diarrhea. Thus, whereas you may have begun by treating an ear infection with an antibiotic, you end up having to cure a much worse case of diarrhea.

There is a very effective aid to your system used in a few hospitals. When you begin a course of antibiotics that threatens to destroy the entire bacteria population of your intestines, begin a diet that includes generous portions of yogurt or buttermilk. These products contain friendly bacteria called lactobacilli, that help to control the undesired bacteria.

More Serious Bowel Disorders

Suppose you get an attack of diarrhea and are horrified to see that it is covered with blood or mixed with it. If the diarrhea is accompanied by a fever, chances are that you have contacted bacillary dysentery, which is usually effectively managed once you pay a visit to your doctor. If there is no fever, you may have developed a good case of hemorrhoids or a mechanical irritation of the bowel lining. On the other hand, you may have one of the more serious diseases that are outside the scope of this book, diseases such as amoebic dysentery, ulcerative colitis, or even cancer of the large bowel.[16]

Statistics are in your favor that diarrhea with blood will mean a simple case of hemorrhoids, but we will not attempt to aid you in a self-diagnosis. If the bleeding persists, hie yourself off to your doctor who will begin with a few simple tests to determine the cause of the blood. If this book does nothing else, we hope it will get you to see your doctor more quickly when there is a chance of really serious illness. The sooner you pay your doctor a visit, the sooner you will be reassured and healed.

Conclusion

It is the rare person who can go through life without a case of the "trots." It is an even rarer individual who travels south of the equator and does not contract at least one form of enteritis. Diarrhea should be looked upon as nature's way of ridding the body of toxic poison, of regulating the state of affairs in the intestines. Throughout history, people have accepted the complaint as not only necessary but therapeutic. There is no need to succumb to the American hysteria toward all symptoms and rush to your druggist for this week's painkiller or bowel stopper. The diarrhea is a signal that you have overdone something, or that you are in imbalance. To stop the process artificially continues the imbalance. Be courageous. Take a rest from your active life for a day or two. Get some rest, take liquids with sugar and mineral salts, and if necessary, the baking soda drink, and enjoy the sensation of a thorough housecleaning. As we have said, if there is persistent blood in the diarrhea, or if the diarrhea does not begin to clear up in thirty-six hours of this regimen, then call your doctor. In the meantime, just relax and obey nature's laws.

9
Flatulence

If the country's family physicians could vote on the most blatant failure of gastroenterologic research, as reflected in current clinical problems, it seems likely they would specify the inability to aid the patient with the complaint of intestinal gas.

—Eddy D. Palmer, M.D.
Editorial Advisory Board
American Family Physician

Since interpreting symptoms in indigestion is difficult for most physicians, and the condition has heretofore been the province of mystics or basic physiologists, neither patient nor physician usually benefits from an encounter which has as its object the relief of gaseous symptoms.

—Albert Mendeloff, M.D.
Mt. Sinai Hospital of Baltimore

Although symptoms thought to be due to "too much gas" are among the most frequently encountered in medical practice, there has been little scientific study of this problem. For this reason, physicians seldom deal rationally with patients with excessive gas, and instead frequently order studies and prescribe treatment without a clear understanding of the pathophysiology of these symptoms.

—John H. Bond, M.D., and Michael D. Levitt, M.D.
University of Minnesota School of Medicine

He took no more account of the wind that passed from their mouth in words than that they expelled from their lower parts.

—Leonardo Da Vinci

95

"Flatulence" is the polite medical term for having gas. When you swallow anything, whether it be a piece of hamburger, a sip of tea, or your own saliva, you normally swallow air as well. The air passes with the foods into the stomach. This air, or gas, now passes from the stomach into the small intestine, to which is added the normal amounts of gas from the fermentative action of intestinal bacteria on carbohydrates. Finally, in the large intestine, or colon, further fermentation and putrefaction take place.

Sources of Gas

Most normal persons have some gas. In many cases, however, flatulence may increase to the extent to which it causes discomfort and embarrassment, and it is at this point that one should view the complaint as a possible symptom of a more complex problem. There are a variety of possible causes of such excessive flatulence.

Aerophagia

The first, most common cause, is aerophagia, the excessive swallowing of air when eating or drinking.[1] This can begin as a habit of childhood. We chew while speaking, or laughing. We eat quickly to get to the school bus, and then later on, to get to work. Or we eat when we are anxious or angry and inadvertently suck in and swallow air. By adulthood, the habit has become a completely unconscious mechanism that is very difficult to detect in ourselves. Furthermore, some people swallow air purposely in order to induce belching. And some of this air may remain in the gastrointestinal tract and contribute to subsequent flatulence.

The obvious solution to the problem of aerophagia, of course, is that you should simply stop sucking in air while eating. You must be able to recognize the problem, however. Now that you are reading this chapter, begin to watch yourself. Ask a close friend or relative to watch you as you eat, drink, or even chew gum. Have this person stop you each time you are apparently swallowing air. You may be surprised at just how many times during the day you inadvertently take in air as you are swallowing your food.

Lactase Deficiencies

You may be one of the lucky ones. You recognize your problem of excessive air swallowing, correct it, and lo and behold, no more flatulence. Chances are, however, that although correcting this problem may noticeably reduce the gas, you are still troubled by indigestion. What is now left is the excessive fermentation of the foods you eat by intestinal bacteria. You may be one of the people over fifteen years old who begins to have difficulty digesting milk and milk products. Researchers have found that large numbers of people have deficiencies of lactase in adulthood which produces malabsorption of lactose in milk.[2] It is quite simple to test for deficiency. Eat nothing all day to clear your colon of past wastes. Then drink only a glass of milk in the early evening. Watch yourself in some systematic way the next few hours. How much gas do you have? How often do you have it? How intense is it? A few days later, again eat nothing all day, and in the early evening this time have only a glass of buttermilk or yogurt. (Soured-milk products have high lactic-acid contents instead of lactose, and lactic acid is more easily tolerated by those persons with lactase deficiencies.) Again, roughly gauge your gas.

You may go on to repeat these two steps of the test again. If you have a lactase deficiency, however, the degree of difference of flatulence in the two parts of the test will be remarkably great. If you find a lactase deficiency, cut out milk products altogether, or switch to high-lactic-acid products such as sour milk, yogurt, and buttermilk. Make sure, however, that you don't go overboard on heavily fermented (sharp) cheeses which may produce as much gas as nonfermented milk products.

Gas from Polysaccharides

If after controlling your intake of excessive air and milk products, you are still bothered by gas, go on to the next most common source of gas, the polysaccharides contained in some vegetables and fruits which cannot be digested and absorbed by the small bowel and therefore pass into the colon.[3] Beans are known to be the worst culprit: "Beans, beans, the musical fruit, the more you eat, the more you toot." Beans contain oligosaccharides, including stachyose and raffinose, which are made up of several sugars linked by bonds that cannot be split by enzymes in the small intestine. These sugars are fermented by colonic bacteria. Researchers have found a tenfold increase in the volume of flatus produced by beans in *most* individuals, so please don't feel you are unusual. Either reduce your intake of beans, or get used to the gas. Other foods usually found to increase colonic gas are peas, cauliflower, cucumbers, cabbage, broccoli, radishes, brussels sprouts, turnips, peppers, onions, and in excess, garlic. You may also have difficulty digesting apples, apple juice, and whole grains. The high-fiber content of these foods results in greater gas production because of the metabolism by colonic bacteria of undigested cellulose which ferments in the intestine.

Many of you who are reading this book are vegetarians. You all may have greatly increased your intake of high-fiber foods in the hopes of maintaining regularity of your bowels. It is unfortunate, but often true, that the most natural relief of constipation produces greater difficulty with flatulence. Flatulence does seem to increase for some people as they change their diet toward a fiber-rich diet of vegetables, fruit, and grains. If you have the time, energy, and willingness to test the gas-producing qualities of each of these specific foods on your colon, by all means forge ahead, and best of luck to you. Each day, limit yourself to one vegetable or fruit, and measure your flatulence. Medical researchers have developed very effective flatus-measuring tests, collecting the flatus in containers and isolating the various gases, thereby ascertaining the proportions of swallowed air, fermenting milk, and fermenting cellulose.[4] You can develop your own phenomenological testing and measuring devices, as suggested above. By such means you can find out which foods you react to most severely.

Chances are that you have better things to do with your energies, however, and more important, you are most likely getting gas from the entire grouping of high-cellulose foods. Obviously you would prefer not to give up such foods. What can you do when you find out such foods produce your gas? Well, first of all, you can increase your eating of lactic-acid foods such as yogurt and buttermilk, which not only aid your body in digesting milk products, but also aid in digesting high-fiber vegetables by increasing the colonic bacteria. Lemon juice and cider vinegar aid in breaking down the cellulose content to more manageable proportions, and they should be used moderately in all your salad dressings. Predigested vegetables such as sprouted beans, seeds, and grains, should be added to your salads and sandwiches. You might try some of the delicious Oriental pickled vegetables such as Chinese pickled radish, garlic, scallion, plum, etc., and see whether you can tolerate the pickled version of these vegetables more than the raw or cooked version.

You might be interested in cookbooks from Eastern countries for food combinations that are as pleasant to your colon as to your tastebuds. It seems no accident, for example, that the Near Eastern combination of yogurt, dill, garlic, vinegar, and cucumbers produces little or no gas in people who would normally blow out like balloons when eating raw cucumbers in a salad. We have given a series of recipes in Appendix A which utilize the healthful properties of certain lactic-acid foods. They should help your colon to digest those healthful but difficult-to-digest foods. More important, however, we hope you will understand and learn the *principles* of such combinations in order to create your original recipes best suited to your own individual needs and tastes.

Gas from Particular Foods and Food Combinations

Other foods sometimes causing indigestion and gas are fried foods such as french-fried potatoes and onion rings, fish sticks, donuts, and pancakes. Many of you who are health conscious have already learned to avoid pies, cakes, and candies in your diets, but you may now be dismayed to find that you cannot so easily digest such "healthful" concentrated sugars as dried fruits: raisins, dates, figs, prunes, apricots.[5] If you find this to be the case, try at least to dilute the sugars by boiling the dried fruits in water or leaving them overnight in a bowl of warm water or pineapple juice and having a delicious compote in the morning which can help your bowels without the discomfort of gas. In any event, any gas that you experience with dried fruits is tremendously increased by combining the fruits with both starches and fats, so watch your digestive reaction to those delicious granola combinations that look so good on paper.

While we're on the subject of the combinations of different foods, we'd like to stress the fact that large amounts of excessive gas are produced not so much by the undigestibility of *particular* foods as by the undigestibility of particular food *combinations*. If you drink a large glass of orange juice and then eat two slices of bread with butter and jam, you may feel extremely uncomfortable in about an hour. The introduction of the orange juice will lessen the amount of ptyalin in your saliva which is needed for a preliminary breakdown of the starches in the bread. The starches are then swallowed whole, leaving your poor digestive system to do all the work. But since your system is already overworked from the fats of the butter and the sugars of the jam, the result will no doubt be some undigested starches moving to the colon to slowly ferment as you sit there in the office trying to appear nonchalant. Many of your family recipes combine foods poorly (for our modern, overworked, and weakened intestines) but produce only moderate, manageable amounts of gas. Just try to make sure that you're not combining indigestibly *all* the time. You may find that certain combinations are entirely intolerable, but others are not so undigestible. Use your own judgment and the voice of your body as your guide. If you notice that certain combinations of foods consistently cause gas or gastric pain, you should create your own tables of "combinations to be avoided."

The Nature of Gas Bubbles

Now, suppose you have checked out everything we have mentioned thus far, corrected your various excesses, but are still troubled by gas. This brings us to the question of what it means to be troubled in the first place. Researchers have found that some individuals with low quantities of gas complain more vociferously of the discomfort due to gas than others with objectively higher quantities.[6] The pains of flatulence occur largely because large bubbles of gas lodge between the folds of the colon. Some of these folds are larger than others. A relatively large bubble may lodge in a much smaller fold of the colon and give a great deal of discomfort. This is why, when the doctor gives you a serious of rigorous tests and tells you that your quantity of gas is not above average, you nevertheless feel as if your gas is worse than everyone else's gas—your average-size bubbles are accumulating in the smaller folds of your colon. Further, it has been noted that it may be more painful to pass 100 milliliters of gas in a single bubble than 100 milliliters of gas in four 25-milliliter bubbles.

The ease with which bubbles are passed is related to the size of the colon at its different points as well as to its flexibility. Colon size is governed by the tone of its smooth muscle and varies from minute to minute. Therefore, given the fact that you have the gas in the first place, and that our preventive methods have not yet ameliorated your condition, the ease with which the gas is passed is determined by the size of the bubbles and the size and tone of the colon. To resolve such a problem we suggest that you go right back to Chapter 6 and cleanse your colon. Then go to Chapter 4 and begin some of the exercises recommended for better bowel function. This will create greater flexibility of your colon as well as increase the motility which should more gently yet firmly thrust the gas bubbles toward their final exit.

Psychological Factors in Flatulence

Your gas, or rather the discomfort due to gas, may be increased by psychological factors.[7] Are you a worrywart? Do you run to your poor doctor or your handy-dandy medical encyclopedia every time you notice a tremor or a tingle? We have tried to cover some of the aspects of psychosomatic disorders in Chapter 2. Similarly in the case of flatulence, worry about the possible causes of your gas, about cancer, about gallstones, about the similarity of severe bouts of flatulence to symptoms of a heart attack, will no doubt impair your digestive processes even more and lead to even greater indigestion. Studies have further found that anxiety in many individuals leads to excessive compulsive eating, where the problem lies not only with the large quantities of foods suddenly to hit your weary digestive tract, but also with the quite irrational combinations of foods, all of which produce even greater amounts of gas which in turn cause greater anxiety which in turn give way to more eating, *ad infinitum.*

The best thing we can say to you now is just to calm down; take it easy. Chances are that your gas can be lessened little by little just by attending to those things we have been talking about.

As you can see from our introductory quotations, flatulence is the second most exasperating, as well as popular, complaint of patients. We suggest that if you suffer from this complaint, as so many adults do, read over this chapter carefully, take your self-diagnoses and self-help mechanisms step by step, and after a few weeks, if you notice *no* improvement, then by all means throw yourself on your family doctor's patience and ask for your very expensive laboratory workup cum x-rays. You most probably will learn nothing of the causes of your gas, but when *more serious pathological conditions are ruled out* in endoscopic studies, you may very well grow calm enough to improve your digestion all by yourself. (In Chapter 12 we tell you what to expect and what to find out in a visit to your doctor.)

Temporarily Relieving Gas

The first part of this chapter has dealt with the systematic prevention of flatulence. Throughout our book, we stress prevention rather than temporary relief from symptoms, and now, only after discussing all significant preventive approaches to flatulence, we turn to various ways to "relieve" your distress. For the most part, these are temporary means. They should be used in isolated moments of stress, physical sickness, sudden changes in lifestyle, all of which may be accompanied by indigestion and gas, even after all preventive care is taken. We do not advise that these means of relief be utilized for the sake of *maintaining* unhealthy modes of life. We do not by any means wish to make it easier for you to persist in unreasonable food combinations, air swallowing, or screaming at your children at dinner. We wish only to offer you possible sources of *temporary* relief so that you might more effectively and comfortably go about finding a permanent balance in your body through preventive means.

Carminatives

As David Ehrlich reported, "When I was living in India fifteen years ago, I noticed, when I first ate in a bazaar cafe, that on every table was a little dish of seeds. For the first month of my stay, I ignored these little dishes and ate my way through the three or four courses of rice, vegetables, and fish dishes, ending the meal with that heavy feeling that usually precedes the onslaught of intestinal gas. It was the first time I had attempted a diet so high in fiber, and I was consistently having a terrible time of it. Once, after about a month, when dining with an Indian friend, I was asked why I declined that little dish of seeds. I replied that I was having enough gas without adding to it the results of just one more dish I had never had before. My friend burst into laughter, exclaiming, 'Why, David, of course you have this gas; we would all of us Indians have this gas if we did not have little dishes of seeds like this one.' It was then that I finally learned of the carminatives, the herbs that stimulate digestion by causing greater secretion of the gastric juices while decreasing the flow of putrefactive bacteria. By stimulating the motility of the colon, they ease the flow of the bubbles through it and break down the largest gas bubbles into more manageable smaller bubbles. From that time on, I have never ceased to use and recommend such herbs, and in my studies of folk medicine around the world, several of these herbs are repeatedly advocated for relief from flatulence."

Mention of anise, fennel, caraway, dill peppermint, and valerian root recurs around the world from India and the Middle East to the native Indians of North America. And it is no accident that our sophisticated Western after-dinner cordials contain one or more of these herbs in alcoholic solution: Anisette (anise), Crème de Menthe (mint). To our surprise, we have even found that in village pubs of Scotland, little dishes of caraway seeds are served with the mug and pitcher of beer (a long-ago discovered relief for the often noisy digestion of beer?). How often has your apple sauce or apple cider been delicately flavored with cinnamon or cloves? Well, by now you will not be at all surprised to learn that cinnamon and cloves also have a mild carminative effect on the stomach lining, especially, it seems, with the digestion of apple products.

We have found that anise, fennel, and caraway seem to be the most effective carminatives, whether carried in your pocket and eaten as is, or boiled and brewed as a herbal tea, or added to cooked dishes as a delicious flavoring agent.[8] All three are easily available on the spice shelf of your neighborhood supermarket or local health-food store, and in an emergency your host can usually be counted on to supply one or more of these kinds of seeds. Why not carry some seeds in your pocket the way you would otherwise carry a pack of gum or cigarettes? If you've never tried any of these seeds, get some anise seeds first. As you sit back, relax, and chew on a few of these seeds, you may very well be reminded of the taste of licorice twists that you used to relish when you were a bit younger.

In Appendix G we give a listing of carminative recipes, the more complicated herbal remedies you can fix at home. The one we mention here has proved most effective with the greatest number of people. We call it Blahende Tea. (*Blahende* is the German word for flatulence, and may also mean "windiness" or "person who blows." In fact, since so few of one's acquaintances know the meaning of *blahende*, we often find it an acceptable communicative term to use with other health-conscious people in social situations.) The recipe for Blahende Tea is one-third teaspoonful each of valerian root, chamomile, and fennel seed (whole or ground), placed in a cup and filled with boiling water. After five minutes, this is strained, mixed with a bit of lemon and honey, and slowly sipped. If after all the preventive measures your flatulence is not clearing up quickly enough for your patience, and that of the rest of your family, have a nice cup of Blahende Tea after every meal instead of your usual gas-producing dessert, and see if this doesn't make the north winds cease.

Charcoal tablets are sold over the counter in most pharmacies and health-food stores. The most popular brand seems to be Requa. Charcoal tablets have been used in America since colonial times to alleviate the symptoms of gas. They seem to absorb some of the gas, or prevent its creation in excessive putrefaction. If you cannot get to your pharmacy today, or if you want to save your pennies, why not just burn a nice piece of toast and eat it with a few caraway seeds.

Europeans as well as Orientals have found garlic to be an especially effective carminative. Half a clove during or after the meal, either eaten whole or cut into tiny pieces and swallowed (to avoid the smell between the teeth) or added to a salad, may aid your colon. In the interests of social equilibrium, the drug industries of our more sedate cultures have come up with a tablet containing the active ingredients of garlic (allicin) in a form that produces no scent in or on the user. Such tablets often combine garlic oil or powder with powdered parsley. Parsley serves both to aid digestion and also to neutralize the smell of the allicin by means of its chlorophyll. If you cannot or do not wish to participate in or support the new super-business of health foods, simply swallow some garlic with some parsley or cinnamon, and your breath will not be all that offensive. You should be aware, however, that one doctor has advised that some patients with irritable colon may be susceptible to cramps from too much garlic.

There are a number of enzyme tablets and chewing gums sold in health-food stores and pharmacies that may aid in the digestion of carbohydrates or proteins or fats, or all three. The active ingredients may be papain (from papaya) or bromelin (from pineapple) all the way to substances derived from the pancreas and liver of oxen. In Hawaii and the South Seas huge, otherwise "indigestible" festival meals with combinations of foods to stagger the Western imagination may be consumed with little or no gaseous effects. To these meals are added extremely generous amounts of papaya and pineapple, each of which contains enzymes capable of breaking down and aiding the body's assimilation of large amounts of proteins, fats, and cellulose. Unless you find that you have an intolerance to all acid fruits—in which case you should also stay away from papaya and pineapple—you may be able greatly to increase your digestive equilibrium by the addition of these fruits, or their tablet forms, to your diet.

Again, at this point we wish to reiterate and expand on our initial caution. We have known a number of otherwise reasonable and health-conscious people with problems of flatulence who did not take proper preventive measures, but who instead relied on enzymal aids such as the ones we have mentioned. Sometimes the condition is immediately improved and the individual gains enough peace, as well as confidence, to take more control of his eating pattern and to improve his diet and his digestion habits to the point where the enzymes are no longer needed. With others, the enzymes provided an illusory sense of relief and well-being. These individuals gained some relief and confidence, which in turn caused them to take on greater amounts of food and more indigestible combinations. In effect, they were led to *increase* their self-defeating eating habits under cover of the enzymes. They have become dependent on the tablets, weakening their own organic digestive powers and forestalling their need eventually to come to grips with their defective bodily functioning. In one sense, gas is a signal by the body that something isn't being handled in quite the correct way. Listen to this signal. In most cases the remedy is a simple one, and there is no reason whatsoever for you to remain ignorant of it, or once found to put off its utilization. We don't wish to encourage you to dampen your body's signals, and so we again emphasize that these curative methods are meant to be *temporary expedients* only.

With this in mind, we move to our last curative aid. This is a synthetic chemical, produced by our drug industry. We include it only because the medical profession seems to use it. *We do not recommend it*, and we have found no substantial data in medical research to warrant its dissemination. In fact, it seems obvious that a few caraway seeds have proved more effective in time-tested tradition than this chemical, known as Simethicone. Simethicone has been shown in several experiments to have had no effect on the total volume of gas expelled, nor on the number of times the gas is passed, nor on the average volume of gas per passage.[9] It did, however, accelerate the transit time through the intestine for the gas. Used postoperatively with patients undergoing gynecological surgery, gas pain and abdominal swelling were relieved in two or three days instead of the usual four days, by the passage of gas more quickly. Apparently its effect is dependent on its physical properties which change the surface tension of the gas bubbles, allowing them to disperse, thus releasing the gas for easier expulsion. The drug has been used extensively with cattle bloat since the early 1940s. It has been used tentatively with humans since the early 1960s. No side effects have yet been found. Still, you should be aware that the research is preliminary and therefore tentative.

Body Positions Useful for
Relieving Gas Pains

In our research, we came across a curious article written by a young couple working at the McAuley Neuropsychiatric Institute of St.

Mary's Hospital in San Francisco, William and Ardith Blackwell.[10] On the basis of extensive personal experience and observation, they seem to have come up with an effective series of body positions with which postoperative flatulence may be relieved. It is important to realize that these positions will not *end* the gas, but will merely cause its expulsion in a less painful, and quicker, manner. The underlying principle of the positions is that, contrary to the physics and related positions of the bowel movements, gas is lighter than air and hence rises. Therefore the most effective position of the flatulent sufferer is with the buttocks raised above the tummy. One variation of the position, called the "Telephoning Teenager Position" by the Blackwells, has the sufferer lie down on her stomach, with legs bent at the knee and raised, arms crossed in front, with head raised a foot or so off the ground. The other most effective position, the "Knee-Chest Position," has the sufferer crouch down, elbows bent and hands flat on the floor in front of him, knees bent so that the thighs press against the abdomen, with the head somewhat raised.

We see no reason why these positions could not be used effectively by the average gas sufferer, and we welcome your experimentation as well as your letters. Generally, we hope that this book will stimulate more dialogue and information exchange in an increasingly health-conscious public.

All exercise, whether it be running, walking, bending, climbing trees, or playing Ping-Pong, tends to stimulate peristalsis, to break down excessively large gas bubbles and to encourage the kind of positive, healthful state of mind which can better tolerate what appears to be a universal symptom of modern life, and in better toleration, could very well mean a lessening of the symptoms themselves.[11]

10
Hemorrhoids

In its collective wisdom, the U.S. government has spent over 50 billion dollars to study the backside of the moon, an area that has caused no one any suffering. But the same government has not spent one cent to study the backsides of its citizens to find out why they suffer from hemorrhoidal disease and what might be done to prevent their painful piles.

—Leon Banov, Jr. M.D.
Charleston, S.C.

It is generally agreed by most medical doctors as well as folk medicine practitioners that hemorrhoids will afflict most of us "civilized" folk at least once in our lives and probably quite a bit more often.[1] What, precisely, do we mean by hemorrhoids, or its alternate term, piles?

"Hemorrhoid" is a Greek word that is focused on the aspects of bleeding. "Piles" is a Middle English term that may be derived from the Latin *pila*, meaning a ball or pillar, evocative of a protrusion or mass. Both doctors and we common folk seem to use the terms interchangeably, but although both are characterized by an internal or external bulge or blister at the anus, not all instances are accompanied by bleeding.

Most medical writers accept the "varicosity theory" of piles. The rectum and anus are supplied with a multitude of tiny blood vessels. During periods of strain and pressure in this area of the body, such as pregnancy, constipation, straining while moving the bowels, the flow of blood through these vessels is interrupted. The blood collects in these vessels and pushes out against the walls in the weakest, least reinforced sections, causing tiny bulges or piles. Recently, other theories have been put forward, the most notable of which is by Hamish Thompson, consultant general surgeon at Gloucestershire Royal Hospital, England. He claims that there are tiny cushions that serve the function of holding the anus closed. When there is undue straining during a bowel movement, for example, these cushions are displaced downward, causing the piles.

All theories as to the origination of the piles cite straining at bowel movements as the most significant precipitating factor, and most practitioners adhere to the three-degree classification of the developing hemorrhoids:

1. Those which show no obvious symptoms except for small bulges or occasional bleeding.
2. Those which appear at the anus upon defecation but return spontaneously or are easily replaced manually.
3. Those which are *permanently* prolapsed or protruding from the anus, or those which, after replacement into the anus, again protrude when the patient stands up.

In first-degree hemorrhoids, the bulges are either internal (inside the anal canal) or external (outside the canal), and bleeding occurs usually when one strains during a bowel movement. The blood is usually not mixed with the movement, but either coating it (in which case the hemorrhoids are internal) or mostly as a smear on the toilet paper (in which case the hemorrhoids are probably external).

In second-degree hemorrhoids, the piles bulge through the anal opening during the bowel movement. However, they can be made to retract either by flexing the pelvic muscles or by pushing them back in with one's fingers.

Third-degree hemorrhoids are the most serious. Even when they are pushed back, they again fall out. They are constantly irritated by underclothing, causing pain, infection, and unconscious avoidance of further uncomfortable bowel movements. Sometimes the hemorrhoids protruding through the anus are trapped by a contraction of the sphincter muscles, strangulating the blood vessels and causing a greater swelling of the hemorrhoids and intense pain and frequent bleeding.

In the majority of cases of bleeding from the anus as described above, hemorrhoids are present. A visit to your doctor would be wise, however, because in a few instances the bleeding may mean something more serious, such as polyps, diverticulosis, or cancer, diseases we shall cover in Chapter 11. After these possible causes have been ruled out, you can begin to cure and prevent further emergence of your hemorrhoids so that it does not develop into a third-degree case. So, assuming that you have already paid a visit to your doctor, or you find *no blood* in your stool but wish to cure a simple case of hemorrhoids, what should you do next? We have divided our section on prevention and simple cures into five parts: cleanliness, diet, exercise, posture, and emotional state. All are equally important. Any self-treatment should combine all five elements.

Cleanliness

In many parts of the world, customs have developed with the aim of keeping the anus free from the bacteria associated with the bowel movement. The French have the bidet, by means of which one can give the anus a thorough washing. Many Asians wipe their anus with water after the movement. And no doubt most of our readers follow the custom of wiping with toilet paper. All medical practitioners stress the need for cleanliness in the prevention and cure of hemorrhoids, and some go so far as to advocate the use of sitz baths. After the bowel movement, sit in a tub of warm water a few inches deep. Then soap the outside of the anal canal (and *only* the outside), and gently rinse. If your hemorrhoids are not yet causing great pain, chances are that you feel a sitz bath is simply too much trouble for you. In this case, why not just practice a variation on the Indian method. Take a piece of toilet paper, wet it slightly in the sink, wipe yourself clean, and then gently pat yourself dry with a second dry piece. Further, it would be a good idea in general to increase the use of showers and baths in the evening or before you leave for work in the morning.

Diet

Throughout this book, and especially in Chapter 3, we have stressed the need for a diet low in animal protein and high in fruit, vegetable, and grain fiber. Most practitioners and researchers agree that straining at stool is the most common cause of hemorrhoids. There should be no reason at all for straining if your movements are soft and easy. Researchers like Dr. D. P. Burkitt in London have shown that populations of Africa and Asia who consume low quantities of animal protein but high quantities of fiber have one-twenty-fifth the rate of hemorrhoids than do those of us in more "civilized countries."[2] Further, it is known that when natives of Asia and Africa adopt Western eating customs, their rate of hemorrhoids increases considerably. High-animal-protein, low-fiber diets produce small firm movements which necessitate greater straining of the muscles as well as the blood vessels and the anal cushions. Lessening or eliminating animal protein from the diet, with a subsequent increase of fruits, vegetables, and grains, should result in larger, softer stools that pass more effortlessly from the bowels. If you conscientiously adopt the diet recommended in Chapter 3, you will greatly lessen the chances of becoming a chronic hemorrhoid sufferer.

Exercise

Studies have shown that there is a much higher incidence of hemorrhoids in persons with sedentary occupations than in persons with ambulatory occupations.[3] It seems that even the farmer falls victim to the disease, a statistic less surprising when we remind ourselves that our modern-day farmer spends much more time sitting on his tractor than he spends walking from the house to the barn. One study, by a group of Indian scientists, describes the constant sedentary position as giving rise to enormous pressure or strain over the anal region, and subsequent appearance of varicosities in the anus, or hemorrhoids.[4] If you've spent the day ensconced in your favorite chair, reading through our book, we are certainly pleased. However, it would be a good idea now if you placed a marker on the page and gently closed the book. This would be the perfect time for you to take a nice long "ambulatory preventive measure," otherwise known as the common walk, or in more primitive language, "moving your ass," which is certainly to the point.

While you are walking and enjoying either the wealth of nature or the theatrical intricacies of a metropolitan street, try to think of all the occasions in which you might try walking instead of sitting. Remove yourself from the sedentary statistics and you help to remove from yourself an aggravating case of the piles.

Posture

Traditionally, researchers have criticized our upright human posture as contributory to hemorrhoids. When our predecessors got off all fours and stood up, our dynamic circulatory system did not fully adjust and the result has been a human susceptibility to vascular disorders such as varicose veins and hemorrhoids. This theory is amazingly simple and ordered, but it does not at all account for the fact that large populations of Africans and Asians, who similarly no longer walk on all fours, have surprisingly low prevalence of these diseases. Although modern medical research has not focused a lot of attention on such seemingly trivial aspects of human life as the toilet posture, many folk healers and naturopaths have pointed to the difference in toilet posture in various parts of the world as a significant factor in the prevalence of hemorrhoids.[5] Most of the more "civilized" animal-protein, low-fiber eaters are also practitioners of the toilet-seat position, as distinct from the "squatting-over-the-hole" position of the high-fiber-eating natives of the Eastern hemisphere. Let's look at the difference anatomically.

Anything which raises the abdominal pressures forces blood down the anal blood vessels. In most cases of muscular straining, the raised pressure within the anal veins is balanced by the tightening of the sphincter muscles. In straining at a bowel movement, however, there is no balancing (or compensatory) support from the sphincter muscles and the veins dilate. In the traditional squatting position for bowel movements, external pressure from the thighs against the abdomen protects and compensates for increased pressure to the anal veins.

Have you ever traveled to a foreign country and been "inconvenienced" by a hole in the floor instead of a raised toilet seat? Then, maybe after you overcame your initial embarrassment, you happened to experience a more effortless movement than usual. Perhaps you didn't notice that the posture was an important factor in the effortlessness. The next time you are in a secluded country spot, try a little experiment, over a well-dug hole. If you experience a smoother and easier movement, you might reflect over the Western tradition of raised seats which adds so much comfort to our "tired legs" at the expense of our bowels.

Unless you have the energy and raw courage to design and change the structure of your toilet bowl, you would do well to go back to Chapter 5 and adopt some of our suggestions for adaptations to the raised seat. If, on the other hand, you experiment and find the squatting position to solve all problems, and if you subsequently set up your hermitage in the African bush, we look forward to your letters of support.

Emotional State

Medical practitioners as well as psychologists and researchers have characterized the sufferer from hemorrhoids in some of the same ways as they have characterized the sufferer from constipation. Dr. J. P. Partridge, a consultant surgeon in England, reported that "most patients with minor ailments of the anus and rectum, including piles, tend to be introspective. Once malignancy has been ruled out, they will respond to almost any treatment . . . just so long as someone else bothers about their bottoms."[6] We cover the emotional determinants of bowel problems in Chapter 2. Here, we shall only briefly reiterate the description of the hemorrhoid-prone individual. A study done by a group of Indian scientists at the Institute of Medical Sciences in Benares, India, bears out the clinical studies done by contemporary Western psychoanalytic writers. The typical hemorrhoid sufferer was nonvegetarian as opposed to vegetarian, was in the habit of both overeating and taking a contradictory (nonbalanced and badly combined) diet, and most important, was generally in the habit of *"withholding his natural urges."* [7] The "anal personality," in classical Freudian theory, is what we would call in modern-day language a "tight-assed personality" who is highly organized, disciplined, restrained in emotional expressiveness. He withholds his urge to defecate for extremely long periods of time to the point of constipation, and when he does deign to sit on the toilet bowl, there is dependence on a disciplined straining for the movement. [8]

If you see yourself in this description—if, in fact, you are one of our readers who has throughout this book been drawing up lists of rules of bowel behavior, typing them on little index cards, and filing them in either alphabetical or topical order—you are a prime candidate for hemorrhoids. It should be of no small comfort for you to know that the two authors of this book, as members in good standing of the Anal Character Club, have been both prime candidates and victims of hemorrhoids. The simplest antidote is, of course, to relax, loosen up, and stop taking things so very seriously. On the other hand, once such a tight-assed individual sets his mind to changing his destructive dietary and bowel habits, the prognosis is usually very good that he will continue, albeit rigidly, in his newly instituted positive habits. So if you find it too difficult to loosen up, be grateful that once you change negative patterns into positive ones, you are the type of individual who will find it just as difficult to slip back into negative habits.

Medical Treatments

Suppose that after having your doctor rule out more serious disease, you have followed our advice in your diet and toilet habits but now find your hemorrhoids growing increasingly painful. You hesitate to visit your doctor again because you have heard from friends or relatives that sometimes hemorrhoidectomy (surgical removal of the piles) is necessary, and that it is extremely painful. Chances are that unless your piles have advanced to a serious third-degree case, surgery will *not* be used. In first-degree cases, you will be advised to add more bulk to your diet, avoiding constipation or diarrhea, to avoid straining at your move-

ments, and to keep the area clean. For the itching or pain of hemorrhoids, your doctor may prescribe a cream or an ointment. (We advise
you, however, to check with your doctor at *all times* before using such
drugs, as *prolonged use of antibiotics may cause more harm than it
cures.*)

In serious second-degree cases and in many third-degree cases,
there are several nonsurgical treatments that may be used as a preferable alternative to surgery.[9] *Injection therapy*, used more in England
than in the United States, consists of injecting a solution under the skin
of the anal canal that serves to "weld" the tissues together, preventing
the protrusion of hemorrhoids. This is painless and is sometimes quite
effective. *Ligation of hemorrhoids* is the placing of a rubber band
tightly around the piles, causing them to recede. This is one of the least
expensive and simplest treatments, and is becoming quite popular in
the U.S. *Dilation* is a manual loosening and stretching of the anus so
that the hemorrhoidal blood flow may return to normal. Your doctor
may use either his fingers or a specially adapted instrument. This
technique, quite painless and simple, has been used most frequently
with the most effective results. *Cryotherapy* is a new technique of
freezing the piles with liquid nitrogen.[10] Medical reports so far have
shown it to be a cumbersome and expensive treatment that has not yet
been developed to the point where it would be preferable to dilation or
ligation. Zeroid is the trade name for one of the cryotherapy treatments.[11] It consists of a plastic cylinder six centimeters in length and
fifteen millimeters in diameter, containing a mixture of glycols as a gel
which can be frozen for four hours in your freezer. The frozen device is
placed into the rectum, lowering the temperature of the surrounding
tissues while it thaws, usually for five to ten minutes. One medical
writer cited the high costs of the Zeroid device as the greatest deter-
rent to its use.

Finally, in some *very serious* third-degree cases that do not respond
to the above treatments, surgery will be advised. This usually means at
least five days in the hospital with at least three weeks, often longer, in
bed. There is a good deal of pain during this period—not as much as
our modern-day myths have created for us, but nevertheless enough
pain and expensive hospital care to make early prevention and treatment of utmost importance.

Anal tags are irregular growths of skin around the anal opening. They are usually the result of minor piles that have receded and healed leaving tiny bits of scar tissue. They neither bleed nor give pain. They will become a problem *only if* they become large in number, because this will make it difficult to wipe properly with toilet paper. If not properly cleaned, they become irritated and cause itching known as pruritis ani (anal itch). If you have scar tissue like this and are unable to keep the area clean, you should pay a visit to your doctor who will remove the tags in a painless and simple operation right in his office.

The vast majority of our readers do not have serious problems with hemorrhoids. When they occur, they will be first-degree cases. Except in the case of bleeding, at which point you should pay a visit to your doctor, your hemorrhoids may be controlled and cured by means of attention to cleanliness, diet, exercise, and emotional relaxation. You are a conscientious person concerned about your health, and by means of these measures, you will not allow your hemorrhoids to develop to the more serious, painful, and expensive stages.

Folk Remedies

There are several folk remedies that have proved effective in curing hemorrhoid sufferers around the world. Although we do not feel that these remedies are any more ridiculous than are the creams and ointments sold over the counter at your neighborhood pharmacy, we do *not* recommend that you experiment with them (just as we do not recommend that you become an over-the-counter suppository addict). We include these descriptions for your interest and curiosity only.

In the Russian Caucasus, for many years suppositories the size of a finger were carved or cast in ice, smoothed over so as not to cause irritation, and left in the anus for thirty to ninety seconds at a time once a day.[12] After improvement began, cold compresses were sufficient. You may think this quite a curious treatment until you are reminded of the newest treatment of "modern medicine" called zeroid, mentioned earlier.

Another series of remedies from the Caucasus involves the application of steam to the piles. Water is boiled and poured into a pan. The pan is covered with a plank into which a six-inch hole has been bored. The sufferer sits on the plank directly over the hole for about half an hour at a time. The variations are due to the particular substances one chooses to boil. In one remedy, half a pound of alum is boiled with two gallons of water. In another, four unpeeled onions are boiled in two quarts of milk. In a Tibetan variation, hooves of animals (goat and Yak) were boiled in water. In each of these variations, Vaseline is smeared on the anus after the steambath.

In Eastern Europe, for hundreds of years suppositories have been made from fresh potatoes, and allowed to remain throughout the day. Pulped carrot, applied either warm or cold as a poultice, may remain for three hours at a time.

In India, the fruit and juice from the seeds of the papaya are given orally to relieve piles as well as constipation.[13]

In agreement with most medical practitioners, almost every folk healer consulted as to prevention and cure of hemorrhoids stressed the need for cleanliness, a preponderance of fruit and vegetables in the diet, and relaxation and nonstraining during the bowel movement. Several commented that if such things were attended to, even our ridiculous raised toilet seats would not bring forth into the world a new hemmorrhoid. So, again, as we have said so many times throughout this book, the best way to avoid bowel complaints is to relax and enjoy yourself.

11
An Overview of the Range of Other Bowel-related Issues

In this chapter we will traverse a broad range of issues going from some of the relatively innocuous to some of the more serious.[1] We make no attempt to be comprehensive here because serious illness is not the topic of this book. In Chapter 12, we shall attempt to clarify for you those times when you should get in touch with your doctor.

Pruritis Ani

This disorder is truly irritating. And we're sure every reader has some familiarity with it, namely, the terribly bothersome ticklish-itchy sensation in the anus.[2] The insistence of the anus to be scratched is undeniable. This disorder is seen more commonly in men than in women. The ratio is about four to one. Sometimes the scratching causes more problems than the initial one, which caused the itching in the first place. The causes seem to be chemical toxins from damaged skin or from the blood circulation which irritate the delicate nerve endings.

Resisting scratching is very difficult for two reasons. First of all, the irritation can be intolerable, and second, the reinforcement from scratching is so gratifying. People have been known to scratch so hard that they tear the skin . . . or to pour strong astringent solutions like alcohol on the affected anus because the itch is absolutely intolerable and any pain is preferable to it. The problem is that these abuses of the skin further injure it and perpetuate the itch-scratch cycle. One of the ways of preventing scratching is to apply a local antiseptic cream prescribed by your doctor.

One of the main causes of the itching is perianal moisture, which irritates the anal skin. This can come from many sources: leakage from the anus, drainage from inflammations, mucus-producing polyps or tumors. Drugs such as quinidine and colchicine may irritate the gut and precipitate pruritis ani. Ingestion of mineral oil has been associated with pruritis, and it may be due to perianal seepage of the oil and feces.

The milk drinker may have a constipated or pasty stool which seeps after the bowel movement is completed. Of course, chronic diarrhea will tend to produce seepage and cause anal itching. Aside from these moisture-induced causes of pruritis ani, skin trauma can be another cause. This can be induced by improper wiping, and friction injury when the patient has much hair sourrounding the anus. Jogging may irritate the anus. Too-vigorous or too-frequent washing may irritate it, too. Some factors often associated with pruritis are nervousness and fair skin.

Early treatment by your doctor probably will involve minimal education and should emphasize preventive measures. If the skin is very lacerated or torn up, the doctor generally prescribes wet packs or soaks, to remove crusts and discharges. Then lotions are put on to dry the area. It is most important that the perianal skin be kept clean, dry, and slightly acid. Sometimes it helps to wear a small piece of cotton to absorb moisture.

Usually these treatments are sufficient to relieve the symptoms. More heroic treatments such as surgery are called for in only a tiny percentage of the cases. In the majority of cases, simple management will clear up the condition. We include a partial list of instructions offered by two University of Oregon Medical School professors.[3] If the condition worsens, you should definitely call your doctor.

1. You should keep the anal area clean and dry and should not wipe too much lest you cause irritation.
2. Do not use too much soap on the area. Soap is alkaline and neutralizes the acid nature of the skin.
3. After bowel movements, pat dry with a moist cotton or tissue.
4. During the day, you may wear a thin wad of cotton dusted with baby powder. Change the cotton as often as it becomes moist.
5. Dietary items that may be related to bowel irritation are citrus fruits and juices, coffee (regular and decaffinated), beer and other alcoholic drinks, nuts, milk, popcorn, and any other regularly gas-producing foods.

Creams and lotions may be prescribed by your doctor in the event that the above simple measures do not relieve your condition. You should not use any medication without consulting with your doctor first.

Mechanical Injuries

The main cause of mechanical injuries to the anus and colon is the insertion of objects during acts of anal-sexual eroticism.[4] There has not been much literature by medical practitioners on anal eroticism. We were therefore heartened in the last months of our research by a timely article by the chief of colon and rectal surgery at Brooklyn Hospital, Dr. A. W. Marino, Jr. We include his introductory comments, which are quite to the point: "Anal sexual eroticism is a fact of modern life. While it is a minor variant in heterosexual intercourse, it is a major part of the male homosexual relationship."[5] But since the anus was not designed to contain the objects which are inserted into it in sexual play, injuries of more or less severity may result.

Traumas can include ulceration or tearing due to anal intercourse, as well as the insertion of foreign bodies. In some cases, such ulcerations may be similar to the symptoms of venereal disease and the doctor may give you a test for these diseases. In most cases of minor ulceration of both the anal canal and the rectum, the doctor will advise no specific treatment beyond the avoidance of reinjury. Much more serious trauma can be inflicted by the insertion into the rectum of a wide range of objects in the practice of anal eroticism. Brooklyn Hospital reported patients entering the emergency ward with the following objects pushed into and "lost" in the rectum: penis-shaped vibrators, a large salami, a ten-inch carrot, broomsticks, whip handles, and compressed-air hoses. Those of you who anticipate the use of such things should understand the great danger they present to your organs: extensive proctitis, perforation of the splenic flexure, rectosigmoid, etc. Equally serious a danger is posed by "fisting"—the insertion of the fist and forearm into the anus of a willing or unwilling subject.

Some doctors in metropolitan areas feel that these kinds of problems are increasing in occurrence, and that the embarrassment associated with them is preventing the dissemination of information that might serve to prevent their occurrence. We hope that we have provoked and initiated the discussion of such things.

Irritable Bowel Syndrome

This syndrome names more what it is not than what it actually is. When there is a disorder of bowel habits generally involving prolonged diarrhea, and sometimes associated with abdominal pain or discomfort, but there is no evidence of disease, infection, tumors, or hormonal imbalance in the body, then you have irritable bowel syndrome.[6] It means that the cause is uncertain. As we said in Chapter 8 on diarrhea, don't look to this book for appropriate treatments for chronic diarrhea problems. It is beyond our scope to discuss medical treatments, and so we repeat, pay your doctor a visit.

From this point on we shall be talking about extremely serious disorders. We have no advice to give you except to see your doctor if you find any indication of the symptoms we describe, especially bleeding from the rectum, and of course severe and persistent abdominal pain of any kind.

Bleeding Rectum

Anorectal bleeding can be a sign of hemorrhoids, or breaks in the wall of the anus (fissures), or of more serious diseases such as cancer and inflammatory bowel disease.[7] By far the most frequent cause is hemorrhoids and fissures close to the anal opening. The proctologist can identify these causes simply by direct visual and manual inspection. However, in about 15 percent of cases the bleeding is due to more serious problems, involving cancer or inflammations of the large intestines. In this case the diagnosis requires the use of a sigmoidoscope, an instrument which can be inserted deep into the colon through the rectum and which allows the physician to look at the walls of the intestines, using the instrument like a flexible periscope. This is often supplemented by a barium enema which reveals the intestines in x-ray pictures. Now let's look at each of the serious disorders of the bowels of which bleeding of the rectum may be just one symptom.

Inflammatory Bowel Disease

Inflammatory bowel disease seems to be on the increase and includes the well-known disease of ulcerative colitis. It is most common in urban populations and attacks young people between fifteen and thirty-five years of age. There are various types of inflammatory disorders. Some involve a breakdown of the intestinal walls. Some involve the thickening of the walls and scar-like growths on the walls. Cracking of the walls and ulcerations may also occur. The symptoms include bleeding, frequent irregular bowels, and abdominal pain. Very often, these diseases require surgical treatment.

Diverticular Disease

Diverticuli are pockets which develop in the walls of the intestine. They are something like the appendix. It's not clear what causes them—possibly an important factor is high pressure inside the colon, as happens with chronic constipation. Problems occur when the diverticuli become inflamed or perforate.

Tumors in the Lower Bowel

Most tumors of the colon are benign, and are called polyps. Polyps look strangely enough, a bit like the atom bomb mushroom cloud we have all seen in pictures. They are rooted in the wall of the intestines, and they are composed of intestinal cells. If they grow too big, they can cause obstructions in the intestines, and ulcerations. Otherwise, they are innocuous.

Malignant tumors are not common in people under forty years of age. There are two definite conditions which are prone to development of carcinoma. The more common one is polyps and the less common one is the ulcers of ulcerative colitis. We cannot repeat enough that you should not be afraid to visit your doctor if you suspect the presence of a tumor in your intestines. The advances in medical research are proceeding at a reassuring rate. And more and more simple and reliable treatments are available every year.

12
Your Doctor—
The Rectal
Examination

By now you should have a clear idea of when to supplement self-treatments and preventive measures by getting in touch with your doctor.[1] Let's review things just to make sure. You should call your doctor if:

1. Bleeding persists for longer than two or three days despite your own treatment.

2. Diarrhea persists for longer than a few days.

3. There is severe and persistent abdominal pain of any sort.

4. There is any definite change in your accustomed bowel habits that does not clear up within a couple of weeks.

5. Constipation persists for two weeks despite following our recommendations.

Furthermore, persons over forty-five should undergo routine physical examinations for the detection of cancer once every two years. Persons over fifty-five should have annual examinations.

As we said at the beginning, our book is not meant to be a substitute for your doctor, but merely an adjunct to his work. Your doctor has access to a multitude of diagnostic techniques by which the precise nature of your disorder may be determined. Our book is meant to guide you in taking charge of your own health, in the maintenance of preventive measures that should keep your body in such a healthy condition that an emergency visit to your doctor is not called for. However, if symptoms persist, and you do pay a visit to your doctor, there is absolutely no reason for you to abdicate control of your own health. In fact, the doctor's job will be much easier and more effective if you are able to aid him in his diagnosis by a clear and reasoned description of your symptoms.

You should be prepared to give a general history of your bowel disorders, especially if this is your first visit to the doctor. You should be able to report past incidence of diarrhea, constipation, hemorrhoids, bleeding, or pain in the rectum or abdomen. And you should report all minor and major surgery you have had. Then the doctor will ask, simply, what the problem is. You will be able to aid your diagnosis invaluably if you can describe your symptoms as precisely as possible. If you have been bleeding, is the blood bright red or brown, or even black? Does the blood drip into the toilet after your bowel movement or is it mixed with the feces? How much blood is there? How often? How long has this condition existed?

If there are pains, where are they situated, how often do they occur, and how long has the condition existed? If there has been prolonged constipation, how long has it existed? Is there pain or bleeding associated with it? What has your diet been? What is the nature of the feces that are finally passed? Have you been taking laxatives? (It is reported that many patients are embarrassed to admit to a laxative habit. If you maintain such a habit, despite our warnings, you should *most certainly* tell your doctor about it!) If you have had diarrhea that persists over a period of time, be prepared to explain how often the movements occur, the color and consistency of the feces, and whether pain or blood accompanies.

Besides aiding the doctor in his diagnosis by a thorough description of your complaint, you can and should lend full and active support to the digital and proctoscopic examinations. We go into some detail concerning the full examination simply because of the anxieties most people feel about it. It is our opinion, and that of many doctors, that these anxieties can be alleviated by your understanding more clearly what is involved in the examination.

The examination of your bowels has been called proctosigmoidoscopy, proctoscopy, sigmoidoscopy, and endoscopy of the lower bowel.

We shall use the term "rectal exam" to describe the visual inspection of the anal and perianal areas, the manual examination of the anus and rectum, and the visual examination of the colon by means of a proctoscope, anoscope, or fiberoptic instruments. The exam may be conducted by your regular family doctor (internist) or you may be referred to a specialist in the area, called a proctologist.

When you make your appointment, be sure you are clear about any preparations you should make prior to the examination. Some specialists advise you not to eat the evening before, or to take an enema the night before your visit so that the lower part of the bowel is cleansed and ready for visual inspection. Other doctors prefer to examine you without cleansing the bowel. They feel that they can learn something by the character of the feces still lodged in the bowel. In the majority of cases, your doctor will administer a commercially made enema right in the office.

For the proctoscopic exam, you will be placed in any one of three positions: the Sims position, the knee-chest position, or the inverted position. The Sims position is most often used if the patient is ill. In the inverted position, which is used most frequently, the patient lies on a standard proctoscopic examining table which can be adjusted to fit the needs of both the patient and the examining physician.

It is extremely important to this exam that you fully cooperate with your doctor. Most doctors are sensitive to the anxieties a patient may have about the discomforts and embarrassment of this exam, and will do their best to lessen them. You will be told why the exam is necessary and exactly what is to happen each step of the way. For example, if you are in the inverted position on the examining table, the doctor may say, "Okay, I'm going to tilt the table forward now. You won't fall. Don't change your position."

First will be the digital examination. The area around the anus will be inspected for hemorrhoids and lesions. Then the doctor may say, "I'm going to insert a finger in the anus. There will be very little discomfort if you do not resist. Just relax." The doctor will insert his finger, which is covered with an examining glove or finger cot, and will gently probe in a sweeping motion in search of abnormalities in the lower rectum.

After the digital examination, your doctor will insert a proctoscope. A lubricant is placed on the anus and the doctor will explain what he is doing. "I am going to insert an instrument called a proctoscope into the rectum. The instrument is about the same size as my finger. It won't hurt a bit if you don't tighten your muscles. Just continue to breathe slowly through your mouth." Your doctor will then slowly insert the proctoscope into the upper part of the rectum and at this point may say something like "I can understand you must have a feeling of fullness which may seem like a need to move your bowels. Don't worry, this is just because the proctoscope is in the rectum. Even though you feel you want to tighten your muscles, please try not to do so, and you will feel much less discomfort. Just continue breathing slowly through your mouth."

As the proctoscope is advanced into the lower part of the colon you will feel somewhat more discomfort or cramps. A doctor sensitive enough to your discomfort may say, "Yes, I understand that there is some pressure in the lower part of your abdomen, but it'll all be over in a moment and you can reduce the discomfort by relaxing and not tightening your muscles." As the proctoscope is drawn out of the bowel, most of the detailed examination is carried out. You may feel at this point as if your bowels are moving, but it is only the sensation of the departing proctoscope.

Depending on your symptoms and on what your doctor finds in the digital and proctoscopic examinations, he may make a further examination with an anoscope, which probes a bit lower down in the rectum than does a proctoscope. He may also take samples of your feces for a microscopic examination or a tiny sample of tissue obtained by a simple rectal biopsy. You may further be given a barium enema x-ray examination. In most cases, however, the first two stages of examination are sufficient to reveal whether or not there is some more serious disorder of the bowels.

In the vast majority of proctoscopic examinations, there is little or no discomfort. The degree of discomfort is directly proportionate to the tightness of your muscles during the exam. And the tightness is a result of your anxiety, embarrassment and sense of vulnerability. We mentioned earlier that your cooperation in this examination is of utmost importance to its effectiveness. It is also extremely important to the absence of discomfort. You must be the one to relax your mind and your abdominal muscles. Presumably, through practicing some of the exercises outlined in our book, you should have no problem relaxing your muscles during the examination. You might read over this chapter before your examination. Make sure you fully understand and can anticipate calmly what the examination will be like. Then go for a nice long walk in the park, do some breathing exercises or anything else that you have found that relaxes you. Now you are ready to work with the doctor toward the diagnosis and cure of your disorder. Don't hesitate to ask your doctor questions about his examination if he does not think to volunteer the information. Cooperate fully and continue to take an active and not a passive role in your own health. Your doctor is an expert in his field. But he is also able to be a friend and an advisor in your personal physical and mental growth.

13
Summary of the Lifestyle and Habits Conducive to Optimal Bowel Functions

In our final chapter, we will briefly review all we've said so far. Reading the entire book has given you a fuller understanding of the importance of healthy and effective elimination, and it has also shown you the many ways by which your elimination may be either aided or hindered. If you've valued the book enough to read it through, then you no doubt value your health in general and your eliminatory processes in particular. It is now up to you to put all your newly found information and conclusions into practice. It is never easy to change one's habits, whether they be dietary, emotional, exercise, or bowel habits. But if there is a commitment to change, if you truly choose to steadily improve your bowel health, you will succeed.

Many people have told us that just doing a few of the things mentioned in this book has caused great improvement in bowel habits. One woman who had suffered from chronic constipation simply added raw bran to her diet and began taking long walks to buy her newspaper every morning. *Within one week*, she had become so regular that she threw her little laxative pills into the toilet. An elderly man who had suffered from flatulence for a number of years began to combine his foods more carefully and switched from milk to yogurt. Within a few days he noticed a real lessening in the amount of gas passed, and within a month he had to be reminded that gas had ever been a problem. What is striking about these cases and others like them is that the sudden noticeable improvement in bowel health acted as tremendous positive reinforcement for further changes in habits. The woman who had added bran to her diet with such positive results soon began to increase her intake of fruit and vegetables, and similarly gradually increased the length of her walks, and her enjoyment of them. The man whose flatulence had all but disappeared also began even greater changes in his diet and soon noticed great improvement in his hemorrhoids.

One of the most positive aspects of bowel disorder is that you can see improvement so quickly and so graphically when you begin to deal with its causes. Remember that laxatives, hemorrhoidal ointments, binding agents, and even carminatives do not deal with the causes of disorders—*they deal with the symptoms*. They offer "symptomatic relief" as the TV ads so truthfully report, and you can bet your bottom dollar that those same symptoms will return again and again until and unless you begin to treat their causes. The causes are improper diet, inadequate exercise, inappropriate coping with emotional stress, and faulty toilet habits. Unless you take charge of these aspects of your life, nothing you buy in your corner drugstore is going to have a real effect on your health. But when you do *begin* to take charge of your life, to respect the totality of your body and mind, the initial improvements and sense of accomplishment will motivate you to continue to remold your habits. The process is not unlike the creative process of the artist. You are the artist, and your body—your total body—is your work. Little by little you mold it, polish it, refine it, until it approaches as nearly as possible the image of perfection in your mind's eye. It will not happen overnight. No great artistic work ever does. But the process of growth of the work is reward in itself. The process, the positive development of your total self step by step, is exquisitely rewarding, and once begun, simply *begun*, it will spur you on to further and further refinement. We ask you only to begin.

We offer below, a list of steps you may take in the refinement of your bowel health. You may already have taken some of these steps before reading this book, or perhaps you had been thinking of taking some of these steps but needed the extra prod. If so, you are already on your way. We include twenty suggestions. They have appeared elsewhere in the appropriate sections of this book and are here grouped together as a single unit. We wished to do this both as an expression of the totality of your mind and body and also as a strategic convenience to you.

You might choose to follow a few of our suggestions for a week or so. After you become comfortable with them, take on one or two others and try to develop these without losing the momentum you gained in the first few steps. Take it slowly and gradually, but persevere. You will find that your strength and sense of well-being improves along with your bowel health. You may also find, as so many others have that success in changing your habits in this sphere leads to the confidence to effect change in other aspects of your life, aspects that you always felt were resistant to change.

We'd like to know what happens. We are planning on a follow-up edition of this book, and in addition to the newest medical research in the area, the reports of improvement in your bowel health after the institution of particular changes would be of great value to us. Each of you who takes charge of your own life and your own health becomes the expert. The process of your steps toward better health will be of great value to other people just like you. Talk to your relatives and friends. Write to us. We hope, finally, that we have begun the dialogue, so long needed, on bowel health.

Toward Better Bowel Health

1. Eat one ounce of raw bran daily.

2. Eat at least one full serving daily of a whole-grain dish.

3. Cut down completely on refined white bread, flour, cake, and pasta.

4. Eat at least two servings of raw or cooked vegetables daily.

5. Eat at least one pint of yogurt or sour milk daily.

6. Eat at least one pound of raw fruit every day.

7. Cut down on all use of sugar, and eat an ounce of honey daily.

8. Add garlic, sprouts, and seaweed to your diet.

9. Take vitamin A (cod liver oil) and B Complex (brewer's yeast) daily.

10. Chew each mouthful slowly and thoroughly.

11. Eat all meals in a relaxed setting.

12. Do not overeat.

13. Take daily exercise and walks.

14. Develop and maintain a comfortable and effective toilet posture.

15. Make sure there is enough time to relax at the toilet.

16. Express your feelings more and "loosen up."

17. Gradually empty the contents of your medicine cabinet into the toilet, with all laxatives the first to go.

18. See your doctor for regular checkups and give him a call if there is an onset of *persistent*, definite symptoms such as diarrhea or bleeding that do not clear up promptly.

19. Develop some form of meditation and/or deep-breathing exercises.

20. Take pleasure and pride in your bowel health.

References

1. How the Gastrointestinal System Works

1. The information in this chapter was drawn in part from P. B. Beeson and W. McDermott (eds.), *Cecil-Loeb Textbook of Medicine* (Philadelphia: Saunders, 1963); T. R. Harrison, *Principles of Internal Medicine* (New York: McGraw-Hill, 1977); and F. A. Jones, J. W. P. Gummar, and J. E. Lennard-Jones, *Clinical Gastroenterology* (Philadelphia: Davis Publications, 1968).

2. The Psychology of Eliminatory Processes

1. This general discussion of psychoanalytic theory was drawn from P. C. Kuiper, *A Psychoanalytic Survey* (New York: International Universities Press, 1972); and J. Strachey (ed.), *The Standard Edition of the Complete Psychological Works of Sigmund Freud* (London: Hogarth Press, 1957).

2. E. H. Wender et al., "Behavioral Characteristics of Children with Chronic Nonspecific Diarrhea," *American Journal of Psychiatry 133*, no. 1 (January 1976): 20–25.

3. C. Illingworth and H. Dew, "The Colon and the Psyche," *The Lancet*, November 24, 1962, p.1098.

4. A. W. McMahon et al., "Personality Differences Between Inflammatory Bowel Disease Patients and Their Healthy Siblings," *Psychosomatic Medicine 35*, no. 2 (March-April 1973); 91–103.

5. See, for example, W. T. Grace, *The Human Colon* (New York: Hoeber Co., 1951); G. L. Engel, "Studies of Ulcerative Colitis: III. The Nature of the Psychologic Processes," *American Journal of Medicine 19* (1955): 231–56; F. Feldman et al., "Psychiatric Study of Consecutive Series of 19 Patients with Regional Ileitis," *British Medical Journal 4* (1967): 711–14; D. T. Fullerton et al., "A Clinical Study of Ulcerative Colitis," *Journal of the American Medical*

Association 81 (1962): 463–71; A. I. Mendeloff et al., "Illness Experience and Life Stresses in Patients with Irritable Colon and with Ulcerative Colitis," *New England Journal of Medicine 282* (1970): 14–17; S. Byrne, "Hypnosis and the Irritable Bowel: Case Histories, Methods, and Speculations," *American Journal of Clinical Hypnosis 15* (April 1973): 263–65.

3. Your Diet

1. Quoted in A. M. Connell, "Natural Fiber and Bowel Dysfunction," *American Journal of Clinical Nutrition 29* (December 1976): 1427–31.

2. Quoted in "Fiber and Moral Fiber," *British Medical Journal 2* (June 1974): 457–58.

3. See, for example, G. R. Cowgill and A. J. Sullivan, "Further Studies on the Use of Wheat Bran as a Laxative," *Journal of the American Medical Association 100* (1933): 795; L. W. Parsons, "Studies of Fiber as a Factor in Intestinal Function," *Journal of the American Dietetics Association 12*(1936): 11; G. A. Williams, "A Study of the Laxative Action of Wheat Bran," *American Journal of Physiology 83* (1927): 1.

4. D. P. Burkitt, "Varicose Veins, Deep Vein Thrombosis, and Haemorrhoids: Epidemiology and Suggested Aetiology," *British Medical Journal 2* (1972): 556; id., "Dietary Fibre and 'Pressure Diseases,' " *Journal of the Royal College of Physicians of London 9*, no. 2 (January 1975): 138–46; id. and P. A. James, "Low-residue Diets and Hiatus Hernia," *The Lancet 2* (1973): 128–30.

5. S. Graham and C. Mettlin, "Diet and the Colon Cancer," *American Journal of Epidemiology 190* (January 1979): 1–20; R. L. Phillips, "Role of Life-style and Dietary Habits in Risk of Cancer Among Seventh-Day Adventists," *Cancer Research 35* (1975): 3513–22.

6. See, for example, J. E. Enstrom, "Colorectal Cancer and Consumption of Beef and Fat," *British Journal of Cancer 32* (1975): 432–38; J. Higginson, "Etiological Factors in Gastrointestinal Cancer in Man," *Journal of the National Cancer Institute 37* (1966): 527–45.

7. V. C. Aries et al., "The Effect of a Strict Vegetarian Diet on the Faecal Flora and Faecal Steroid Concentration," *Journal of Pathology 103* (1971): 54–56; B. S. Reddy and E. L. Wynder, "Metabolic Epidemiology of Colon Cancer," *Cancer 39* (1977): 2533–39; B. S. Reedy et al., "Effect of a Diet with High Levels of Protein and Fat on Colon Carcinogenesis," *Journal of the National Cancer Institute 57* (1976): 567–69; E. L. Wynder, "The Epidemiology of Large Bowel Cancer," *Cancer Research 35* (1975): 3388–94.

8. S. Graham et al., "Diet in the Epidemiology of Cancer of the Colon and Rectum," *Journal of the National Cancer Institute 61* (1978): 709–14; B. S. Drasar and M. J. Hill, *Human Intestinal Flora* (New York; Academic Press, 1974); R. L. Walters et al., "Effects of Two Types of Dietary Fibre on Faecal

Steroid and Lipid Excretion," *British Medical Journal 2* (1975): 536; R. F. Harvey et al., "Effects of Increased Dietary Fibre on Intestinal Transit," *The Lancet 1* (1973): 1278; M. A. Eastwood et al., "Effects of Dietary Supplements of Wheat Bran and Cellulose on Faeces and Bowel Funcion," *British Medical Journal 4* (1973): 392.

9. L. W. Wattenberg, "Studies of Polycyclic Hydrocarbon Hydroxylases of the Intestine Possibly Related to Cancer," *Cancer 28* (1971): 99–102; E. Bjelke, "Epidemiologic Studies of Cancer of the Stomach, Colon, and Rectum, with Special Emphasis on the Role of Diet," unpublished doctoral dissertation, University of Minnesota, 1973.

10. L. W. Wattenberg and W. D. Loub, "Inhibition of Polycyclic Aromatic Hydrocarbon-induced Neoplasia by Naturally Occurring Indoles," *Cancer Research 38* (1978): 1410–13.

11. B. Modan et al., "Low Fiber Intake as an Etiologic Factor in Cancer of the Colon." *Journal of the National Cancer Institute 55* (1975): 15–18; S. Graham et al., "Diet in the Epidemiology of Cancer of the Colon and Rectum," *Journal of the National Cancer Institute 61* (1978): 709–14.

12. J. B. Wyman et al., "The Effect on Intestinal Transit and The Feces of Raw and Cooked Bran in Different Doses." *American Journal of Clinical Nutrition 29* (December 1976): 1474–79.

13. Quoted in A. R. P. Walker, "Colon Cancer and Diet, with Special Reference to Intakes of Fat and Fiber," *American Journal of Clinical Nutrition 29* (December 1976): 1422.

14. Drasar and Hill, *Human Intestinal Flora.*

15. Walker, "Colon Cancer and Diet."

16. Wyman et al., "The Effect on Intestinal Transit and the Feces of Raw and Cooked Bran in Different Doses"; Eastwood et al., "Effects of Dietary Supplements . . ."

17. J. F. Dastur, *Medicinal Plants of India and Pakistan* (Bombay: D. P. Taraporevala Sons & Co., 1962); L. Harris, *The Book of Garlic* (New York: Holt, Rinehart &Winston, 1975); R. Lucas, *Nature's Medicines* (New York: Award Books, 1966), pp. 40–68; T. Watanabe, *Garlic Therapy* (Tokyo: Japan Publications, 1974); A. Bordia and H. C. Bansal, "Essential Oil of Garlic in Prevention of Artherioschlerosis," *The Lancet*, December 29, 1973, p. 1491; C. J. Cavallito, "Allicin, the Anibacterial Principle of Allium Sativum," *Journal of the American Chemical Society 66* (1944): 1950–51; E. E. Marcovici, "Garlic Therapy for Digestive Disorders," *Medical Record 153* (January 1941): 63–65; E. Weiss, "A Clinical Study of the Effects of Desicated Garlic in Intestinal Flora," *Medical Record 153* (June 1941): 404–408; M. G. Johnson and R. H. Vaughn, "Death of Salmonella Typhimurium and Escherichia Coli in the Presence of Freshly Reconstituted Dehydrated Garlic and Onion," *Applied Microbiology 17* (June 1969): 903–905; G. J. Bastidas, "Effect of Garlic," *American Journal of Tropical Medicine 18* (November 1969): 920–23.

18. M. Levitt and J. Roth, "In Consultation: Gas in the Gut," *Medical World*

News 16, no 8 (April 21, 1975): 92–107; H. Seneca et al., "Bactericidal Properties of Yoghurt," *American Practitioner and Digest of Treatment 1* (1950): 1252–59; J. N. Rosell, "Yoghurt and Kefir in Their Relation to Health and Therapeutics," *Canadian Medical Association Journal 26* (1932): 341.

19. P. N. Durrington et al., "Effect of Pectin on Serum Lipids and Lipoproteins, Whole-gut Transit-time, and Stool Weight," *The Lancet*, August 21, 1976, p. 344; H. W. Haggard and L. A. Greenberg, "Influence of Certain Fruit Juices on Gastric Function," *American Journal of Digestive Diseases 8* (1941): 163–70.

20. J. L. Breeling, "Pharmacologic Basis for Cathartic Action of Prune Juice," *Journal of the American Medical Association 209* (1969): 1726.

21. Ibid.; F. G. Saibil, "Factitious Diarrhea," *Canadian Medical Association Journal 111*, no. 10 (November 1974): 1108–1109.

22. N. Yoirish, *Curative Properties of Honey and Bee Venom*, trans. Xebia Dank (San Francisco; New Glide Publications, 1977); *The Hive and the Honey Bee* (Hamilton, Ill.: Dadant and Sons, 1975); M. B. Blomfield, "Honey for Decubitus Ulcers," *Journal of the American Medical Association 224* (1973): 905; M. H. Hyadak et al., "The Role of Honey in the Prevention and Cure of Nutritional Anemia in Rats," *Journal of Pediatrics 26*, no. 6 (1942): 763–68; A. G. Lochhead and D. A. Heron, "Microbiological Studies of Honey," *Canadian Department of Agriculture Bulletin* no. 116 (1929); F. I. Seymour and K. S. West, "Honey—Its Role in Medicine," *Medical Times 79* (1951): 104–107.

23. The information in this section was drawn in part from M. H. Oliver, *Add a Few Sprouts* (New Canaan, Conn.: Keats Publishing Co., 1975); D. M. Adkins, "Digestibility of Germinated Seeds," *Biochemical Journal 14* (1920): 637–41; K. N. T. Wai et al., "The Vitamin Content of Soybeans and Soybean Sprouts as a Function of Germination Time," *Plant Physiology 22* (1947): 117–26; P. R. Burkholder, "Vitamins in Dehydrated Seeds and Sprouts," *Science 97* (1943): 562–64; H. P. Chattopadhyay and S. Banerjee, "Effect of Germination on the Carotene Content of Pulses and Cereals," *Science 113* (1951): 600; L. J. Harris and S. N. Ray, "Specificity of Hexuronic Acid as Anti-scorbutic Factor," *Biochemical Journal 27* (1933): 580; G. S. Hall and D. L. Laidman, "The Pattern and Control of Isoprenoid Quinone and Tocopherol Metabolism in the Germinating Grain of Wheat," *Biochemical Journal 108* (1968): 475–82.

4. Exercising for Better Bowel Function

1. M. J. Takach, *The Right Way to Walk for Health* (New York: Award Books, 1973).

2. M. D. Levitt, "Intestinal Gas," *Postgraduate Medicine 57*, no. 1 (January 1975): 77–81.

3. The information in this section was drawn largely from L. M. Folan, *Lilias Yoga and You* (New York: Bantam Books, 1978); and Yogiraj Sri Swami Satchidananda, *Integral Yoga Hatha* (New York: Holt, Rinehart and Winston, 1970)

5. Toilet Positions and Activities for Making Elimination Easy and Rewarding

1. L. Lambton, *Temples of Convenience* (New York: St. Martin's Press, 1978).

2. Burkitt and James, "Low-residue Diets and Hiatus Hernia"; Burkitt, "Varicose Veins . . ."; D. Cranston and D. P. Burkitt, "Diet, Bowel Behavior, and Disease," *The Lancet 2* (1975): 37; S. S. Fedail et al., "Abdominal and Thoracic Pressures During Defecation," *British Medical Journal* (January 13, 1979): 91; J. A. C. Thorpe, "Abdominal and Thoracic Pressures During Defecation," *British Medical Journal* (February 3, 1979): 344.

6. Periodic Cleansing Techniques

1. For general information on the historical background on the enema, see C. C. Mettler, *The History of Medicine* (Philadelphia: Blakiston Co., 1947)

2. See M. O. Garten, *The Health Secrets of a Naturopathic Doctor* (West Nyack, N.Y.: Parker Publishing Co., 1967), pp. 86–90; "Small Bowel Enemas," *Annales de Radiologie 21*, nos. 2–3 (1978): 143–48.

3. See, for example, Garten, *Health Secrets . . .*; C. Wade, *Health Secrets from the Orient* (New York: Signet Paperbacks, 1974); P. Airola, *Health Secrets from Europe* (New York: Arco, 1978); G. Null and S. Null, *The Complete Handbook of Nutrition* (New York: Dell, 1973).

4. V. Vertes et al., "Supplemented Fasting as a Large-scale Outpatient Program," *Journal of the American Medical Association 238*, no. 20 (1977): 2151–53; E. J. Drenick et al., "Effect on Hepatic Morphology of Treatment of Obesity by Fasting, Reducing Diets, and Small-bowel Bypass," *New England Journal of Medicine 282* (1970): 829–34; E. J. Drenick et al., "Prolonged Starvation as Treatment for Severe Obesity," *Journal of the American Medical Association 187* (1964): 100–105; S. M. Genuth et al., "Weight Reduction in Obesity by Outpatient Semistarvation," *Journal of the American Medical Association 230* (1974): 987–91; D. J. Miletich, "Fasting and Metabolism," *Anesthesiology 47*, no. 2 (August 1977): 235.

5. D. H. Boehme, "Preplanned Fasting in the Treatment of Mental Disease: Survey of Current Soviet Literature," *Schizophrenia Bulletin 3*, no. 2 (1977): 288–96.

6. T. Lawlor and D. G. Wells, "Metabolic Hazards of Fasting," *American Journal of Clinical Nutrition 22* (1969): 1142–49; V. Vertes et al., "Precautions with Supplemented Fasting," *Journal of the American Medical Association 238*, no. 20 (1977): 2142.

7. Constipation

1. For general background on this topic, see F. A. Jones and E. W. Godding (eds.), *Management of Constipation* (London: Blackwell, 1968).

2. C. Illingworth and H. Dew, "The Colon and the Psyche," *The Lancet*, November 24, 1962, p. 1098.

3. See, for example, F. C. Jewell and J. R. Kline, "The Purged Colon," *Radiology 62* (1954): 368–71; G. E. Sladen, "Effects of Chronic Purgative Abuse," *Proceedings of the Royal Society of Medicine 65* (1972): 288–91; W. T. Cooke, "Laxatives and Purgatives," *The Practitioner 206* (1971): 77–80.

4. W. C. Watson et al., "The Absorption and Excretion of Castor Oil in Man," *Journal of Pharmacy and Pharmacology 15* (1963): 183–88.

8. Diarrhea

1. Quoted in A. P. Douglas, "Diarrhoea," *Nursing Times 71*, no. 51 (December 18, 1975): 2022–23.

2. E. J. Gangarosa, "Recent Developments in Diarrheal Diseases," *Postgraduate Medicine 62*, no. 2 (August 1977): 115.

3. See N. Hirschorn and D. Nalin, "Sucrose or Glucose for Diarrhoea," *The Lancet 2*, December 10, 1977, p. 8050; D. Nalin et al., "Comparison of Sucrose with Glucose in Oral Therapy of Infant Diarrhoea," *The Lancet 2*, August 5, 1978, p. 8084.

4. Gangarosa, "Recent Developments in Diarrheal Diseases."

5. See, for general background information, H. L. Bockus (ed.), *Gastroenterology* (Philadelphia: Saunders, 1974); M. H. Sleisinger and J. S. Fordtran (eds.), *Gastrointestinal Disease* (Philadelphia: Saunders, 1973) A. Bogoch, *Gastroenterology* (New York: McGraw-Hill, 1973).

6. See, for example, S. Byrne, "Hypnosis and the Irritable Bowel: Case Histories, Methods, and Speculation." *American Journal of Clinical Hypnosis 15* (April 1973): 263–65.

7. F. G. Saibil, "Factitious Diarrhea," *Canadian Medical Association Journal 111*, no. 10 (November 16, 1974): 1108–1109.

8. L. D. Goldberg and N. T. Ditchek "Chewing Gum Diarrhea," *American Journal of Digestive Diseases 23*, no. 6 (June 1978): 568

9. See J. D. Fryboski, "Diarrhea from Dietetic Candy," *New England Journal of Medicine 275* (1966): 718; R. Pochaczevsky, "Oral Examination of the Colon: The Colonic Cocktail," *American Journal of Roentgenology 121* (1974): 318–25.

10. A. P. Douglas, "Diarrhoea," *Nursing Times 71*, no. 51 (December 18, 1975): 2023; D. R. Bell, "Differential Diagnosis of Diarrhoea in Adults," *The Practitioner 213* (July 1974): 47–53; S. F. Phillips, "Diarrhea: Pathogenesis and Diagnostic Techniques," *Postgraduate Medicine 57*, no. 1 (January 1975): 65–72; I. Buhac and J. A. Blaint, "Practical Therapeutics," *American Family Physician 12*, no. 5 (November 1975): 149–59; T. M. Bayless et al., "Lactose Intolerance and Milk Drinking Habits," *Gastroenterology 60* (1971): 605–608.

11. For general information on traveler's diarrhea, see A. C. Turner, "The Diarrhoeas of Travel," *British Journal of Hospital Medicine 17*, no. 1 (1977): 25–28; B. J. Freeman, "Traveler's Diarrhoea," *British Medical Journal 2*, September 4, 1976, p. 6035; C. T. Huang et al., "Fecal Steroids in Diarrhea, Traveler's Diarrhea," *American Journal of Clinical Nutrition 31*, no. 4 (April 1978): 626–32; T. Chang, "Traveler's Diarrhea," *Annals of Internal Medicine 89*, no. 3 (September 1978): 428–29; H. L. Dupont et al., "Diarrhea of Travelers to Mexico," *American Journal of Epidemiology 105*, no. 1 (1977): 37–41.

12. "Montezuma's Revenge," editorial, *The Lancet 2*, July 3, 1976, p. 30.

13. See, for example, Turner, "The Diarrhoeas of Travel"; M. Troy, *Better Bowel Health* (New York: Pyramid Books, 1974), pp. 92–94.

14. See Phillips, "Diarrhea: Pathognesis and Diagnostic Techniques"; Nalin et al., "Comparison of Sucrose with Glucose . . ."; Gangarosa, "Recent Developments in Diarrheal Diseases"; D. R. Bell, "Acute Diarrhoea in Adults," *British Medical Journal 2* (1976): 1240–42; P. A. Oill et al., "Infectious Disease Emergencies," *Western Journal of Medicine 126*, no. 1 (1977): 32–45.

15. Troy, *Better Bowel Health*, pp. 85–88; W. L. George et al., "Antimicrobial Agent-induced Diarrhea—A Bacterial Disease," *Journal of Infectious Diseases 136*, no. 6 (December 1977): 822–26; R. DeJesus and W. W. Peternel, "Antibiotic-associated Diarrhea Treated with Oral Tetracycline," *Gastroenterology 74* (May 1978): 818–20; T. K. Satterwhite and H. L. Dupont, "The Patient with Acute Diarrhea," *Journal of the American Medical Association 236*, no. 23 (December 6, 1976): 2662–64; H. C. New et al., "Incidence of Diarrhea Associated with Clindamycin Therapy," *Journal of Infectious Diseases 135* (suppl., 1977): S120–25; F. E. Pittman et al., "Colitis Following Oral Lincomycin Therapy," *Archives of Internal Medicine 134* (1974): 368–72.

16. J. T. Williams and J. P. S. Thomas, "Ano-rectal Bleeding: A Study of Causes and Investigative Yields," *The Pracitioner 219* (September 1977): 327–31.

9. Flatulence

1. Mendeloff, "Gaseous Indigestion"; J. L. Roth and H. L. Bockus, "Aerophagia: Its Etiology, Syndromes, and Management," *Medical Clinics of North America 41*, (November 1957): 1673–96; M. D. Levitt, "Intestinal Gas," *Postgraduate Medicine 57*, no. 1 (1975): 77–81; S. Glouberman, "Intestinal Gas," *Arizona Medicine 34*, no. 9 (1977): 618–19.

2. See, for example, J. D. Walsh, "Isolated Lactase Deficiency in Humans: Report on 100 Patients," Medicine 49 (1970): 257; J. H. Bond and M. D. Levitt, "Quantitative Measurement of Lactose Absorption," *Gastroenterology 70* (1976): 1058; Levitt, "Intestinal Gas"; M. Levitt and J. Roth, "In Consulation: Gas in the Gut," *Medical World News 16*, no. 8 (April 21, 1975): 92–107.

3. For background on polysaccharides, see F. R. Steggerda, "Gastrointestinal Gas Following Food Consumption," *Annals of the New York Academy of Sciences 150* (1968): 57–66; F. R. Steggerda and J. F. Dimmick, "Effects of Bean Diets on Concentration of Carbon Dioxide in Flatus," *American Journal of Clinical Nutrition 19* (1966): 120–24; J. R. Wagner et al., "Comparative Flatulence Activity of Beans and Bean Fractions for Man and the Rat," *Journal of Nutrition 107*, no. 4 (1977): 680–89; J. R. Wagner et al., "Hydrogen Production in the Rat Following Ingestion of Raffinose, Stachyose, and Oligosaccharide-free Bean Residue," *Journal of Nutrition 106*, no. 4 (1976): 466–70; E. W. Hellendoorn, "Intestinal Effects Following Ingestion of Beans," *Food Technology 23* (1969): 795–800.

4. Steggerda, "Gastrointestinal Gas Following Food Consumption"; Levitt, "Intestinal Gas"; E. Kirk, "The Quantity and Composition of Human Colonic Flatus," *Gastroenterology 12* (1949): 782; id., "Production and Excretion of Hydrogen Gas in Man," *New England Journal of Medicine 281* (1969): 122–27; J. M. Beazell and A. C. Ivy, "The Quantity of Colonic Flatus Excreted by the 'Normal Individual,'" *American Journal of Digestive Diseases 8* (1941): 128.

5. C. A. Hickey et al., "Intestinal Gas Production Following Ingestion of Fruits and Fruit Juices," *American Journal of Digestive Diseases 9*, no. 2 (1942): 197.

6. Levitt, "Intestinal Gas"; Palmer, "The Colonic Gas Problem"; J. E. Carless et al., "The Effect of Particulate Dispersing Agents on the Antifoaming Properties of Dimethicone 1000 in Antiflatulent Products," *Journal of Pharmacy and Pharmacology 25* (November 1973): 849–53.

7. See Levitt, "Intestinal Gas"; A. I. Mendeloff et al., "Illness Experience and Life Stresses in Patients with Irritable Colon and With Ulcerative Colitis," *New England Journal of Medicine 282* (1970): 14–17.

8. See also M. Troy, *Better Bowel Health* (New York: Pyramid Books, 1974).

9. I. E. Danhof and J. J. Stavola, "Accelerated Transit of Intestinal Gas with Simethicone," *Obstetrics and Gynecology 44* (July 1974): 148–54; W. I. Reinhardt, "Experiences with a Digestant-Siloxane Combination, the

Treatment of Intestinal Gas," *Medical Times* 89 (1961): 1099–1101; J. A. Rider and H. C. Moeller, "Use of Silicone in the Treatment of Intestinal Gas and Bloating," *Journal of the American Medical Association* 174 (1960): 2052–54; Glouberman, "Intestinal Gas."

10. A. K. Blackwell and W. Blackwell, "Relieving Gas Pains," *American Journal of Nursing* 75, no. 1 (1975): 66–67.

11. See Levitt, "Intestinal Gas."

10. Hemorrhoids

1. For general background on hemorrhoids, see J. P. S. Thomson, "Contemporary Surgery, Hemorrhoids, and Fissure," *British Journal of Hospital Medicine* 20 (November 1978): 600–609; J. P. Partridge, "Treatment of Hemorrhoids," *Nursing Times* 71 (June 12, 1975): 928–29; H. Thomson, "A New Look at Hemorrhoids," *Medical Times* 104 (November 1976): 116–23; id., "Piles, Their Nature and Management," *The Lancet* 2, September 13, 1975, pp. 494–95; M. L. Corman et al., "Alternatives to Surgical Hemorrhoidectomy," *Geriatrics* 29, no. 10 (1974): 99–101; C. B. Jones and P. F. Schofield, "A Comparative Study of the Methods and Treatment for Haemorrhoids," *Proceedings of the Royal Society of Medicine 68, no. 9 (1975):* 574–75; L. E. Smith, "How to Treat Hemorrhoids: Five Nonsurgical Alternatives," *Geriatrics* 33, no. 10 (1978): 43–48.

2. D. P. Burkitt, "Hemorrhoids, Varicose Veins, and Deep Vein Thrombosis: Epidemiologic Features and Suggested Causative Factors," *Canadian Journal Of Surgery* 18, no. 5 (1975): 483–88; id., "Dietary Fiber and 'Pressure Diseases,'" *Journal of the Royal College of Physicians of London* 9, no. 2 (1975): 138–46; id. and P. A. James, "Low-residue Diets and Hiatus Hernia," *The Lancet* 2 (1973): 128–30.

3. G. C. Prasad et al., "Studies on Etiopathogenesis of Hemorrhoids," *American Journal of Proctology* 27, no. 3 (June 1976): 33–41; Burkitt, "Hemorrhoids, Varicose Veins, and Deep Vein Thrombosis"; id., "Dietary Fiber and 'Pressure Diseases.'"

4. Prasad et al., "Studies on Etiopathogenesis of Hemorrhoids."

5. See, for example, C. J. B. Muller, "Abdominal Pressures," *South African Medical Journal* 22 (1948): 376; D. P. Burkitt, "Varicose Veins, Deep Vein Thrombosis, and Haemorrhoids: Epidemiology and Suggested Aetiology," *British Medical Journal* 2 (1972): 556; S. S. Fedail et al., "Abdominal and Thoracic Pressures During Defecation," *British Medical Journal 1*, January 13, 1979, p. 91; J. A. C. Thorpe, "Abdominal and Thoracic Pressures During Defecation," *British Medical Journal 1*, February 13, 1979, p. 344.

6. Partridge, "Treatment of Hemorrhoids."

7. Prasad et al., "Studies on Etiopathogenesis of Hemorrhoids,"

8. S. Freud, "Character and Anal Eroticism," in id., *The Standard Edition of*

the Complete Psychological Works of Sigmund Freud, edited by J. Strachey, vol. 10 (London: Hogarth Press, 1957).

9. Smith, "How to Treat Hemorrhoids."

10. R. E. B. Tagart, "Cryotherapy for Piles," *British Medical Journal 4,* October 18, 1975, p. 165; H. D. Kaufman, "Cryotherapy for Piles," *British Medical Journal 4,* November 22, 1975, pp. 463–64; P. F. Schofield and M. Wilson, "Cryosurgery for Piles," *British Medical Journal 4,* November 29, 1975, p. 520; W. W. Slack, "The Role of Cryotherapy in Management of Anorectal Disease," *Diseases of the Colon and Rectum 18,* no. 4 (1975): 282–83.

11. G. B. Paloschi, "Zeroid: Alternative Treatment of Hemorrhoids," *Canadian Medical Association Journal 118,* no. 3 (1978): 235; W. W. H. Rudd, "Zeroid: Alternative Treatment of Hemorrhoids," *Canadian Medical Association Journal 119,* no. 5 (1978): 408.

12. P. M. Kourenoff, *Russian Folk Medicine* (New York: Pyramid Books, 1971), pp.103–109.

13. J. F. Dastur, *Medicinal Plants of India and Pakistan* 2d ed. (Bombay: D. B. Taraporevala & Co., 1962).

11. An Overview of the Range of Other Bowel-related Issues

1. For general background on this topic, see L. Galton, *The Complete Book of Symptoms and What They Can Mean* (New York: Simon and Schuster, 1978); R. W. Wilkins and N. G. Levinsky, *Medicine: Essentials of Clinical Practice,* 2d ed. (Boston: Little, Brown, 1978).

2. E. S. Sullivan and W. M. Garnjobst, "Pruritis Ani: A Practical Approach," *Surgical Clinics of North America 58,* no. 3 (June 1978): 505–10.

3. Ibid.

4. On mechanical injuries, see N. Sohn et al., "Social Injuries of the Rectum," *American Journal of Surgery 134* (November 1977): 611–12; P. Rhodes, "Sex Aids," *British Medical Journal 3* (1975): 93; J. F. Bartizal et al., "A Critical Review of Management of 392 Colonic and Rectal Injuries," *Diseases of the Colon and Rectum 17* (1976): 313.

5. A. W. Marino, Jr., "Anal Eroticism," *Surgical Clinics of North America 58,* no. 3 (June 1978): 513–18.

6. On irritable bowel syndrome, see S. Byrne, "Hypnosis and the Irritable Bowel," *American Journal of Clinical Hypnosis 15* (April 1973): 263–65; "Irritable Bowel Syndrome," editorial, *British Medical Journal,* January 22, 1972, pp. 197–98; A. I. Mendeloff et al., "Illness Experience and Life Stresses in Patients with Irritable Colon and Ulcerative Colitis," *New England Journal*

of Medicine 282 (1970): 14–17; D. A. Drossman, "Diagnosis of the Irritable Bowel Syndrome," *Annals of Internal Medicine 90*, no. 3 (1979): 431–32.

7. See J. T. Williams and J. P. S. Thomson, "Ano-rectal Bleeding: A Study of Causes and Investigative Yields," *The Practitioner 219* (September 1977): 327–31; W. P. Mazier et al., "Anal Fissure and Anal Ulcers," *Surgical Clinics of North America 58*, no. 3 (June 1978): 479–85.

12. Your Doctor—
The Rectal Examination

1. For a general background, see R. Jackson and J. Spencer, *Practice of Medicine* (New York: Harper and Row Medical Department, 1978), esp. Chapter 33, "Proctosigmoidoscopy"; T. M. Talbott and J. M. Mackeigan, "Colonic Endoscopy in Perspective," *Surgical Clinics of North America 58*, no. 3 (June 1978): 459–68; J. S. Abrams, "A Hard Look at Colonoscopy," *American Journal of Surgery 133* (1977): 113; J. A. Coller et al., "Need for Total Colonoscopy," *American Journal of Surgery 131* (1976): 493; M. G. Schmitt et al., "Diagnostic Colonoscopy," *Gastroenterology 69* (1975): 768; C. Williams and R. Teague, "Colonoscopy," *Gut 14* (1973): 990; W. I. Wolff et al., "Comparison of Colonoscopy and the Contrast Enema in Five Hundred Patients with Colorectal Disease," *American Journal of Surgery 129* (1975): 186.

Appendices

Appendices

A
Recipes for a Healthy Elimination

Below we include twenty of our favorite recipes. They are based on a multitude of cooking techniques from throughout the world. Besides being delicious, these dishes will contribute to a healthy elimination and general physical well-being. We hope that your success with these recipes will encourage you to experiment with the creation of your own dishes utilizing such foods as sprouts, seaweed, whole grains, bran, papaya, and yogurt. In fact, we hope that you will share some of your creations with us so that we may use them in the next edition of this book.

Desserts

FRUIT SALAD

1 cup plain yogurt	2 tablespoons honey
6 soaked figs or prunes (pitted)	1 tablespoon brewer's yeast
¼ lb. papaya, apple, or banana	pinch of ground cinammon

Mix together the yogurt, honey, yeast, and cinammon, and pour over the fruit. Serves one.

POLYNESIAN ENZYME SALAD

1 cup pineapple chunks, strained
1 cup papaya chunks
1 cup cored apple chunks
2 ounces alfalfa sprouts
2 tablespoons juice strained
    from pineapple

1 tablespoon cider vinegar
2 tablespoons sesame oil
1½ tablespoon honey

Mix together the oil, honey, vinegar, and juice, and pour over a mixture of fruit and sprouts. Serves three.

PAPAYA DRINK

½ cup papaya or apple juice
2 cups fresh papaya
2 tablespoons yogurt

2 tablespoons honey
½ tablespoon brewer's yeast
½ tablespoon bran

Mix all ingredients in blender. Serves two.

APPLE COMPOTE

5 lbs. apples
½ lb. mixture of dates
    figs, raisins
¼ lb. honey

2 pints apple juice
1 pint water
1 tablespoon cider vinegar
½ tablespoon cinammon

Core apples and cut into half-inch pieces. Set aside. Pour water and juice into a large pot. Add apples and cook over a medium flame until the apples soften (15–20 minutes). Add the other ingredients, and cook over a low flame for an additional 20 minutes, stirring occasionally. Serves four.

APPLE COMPOTE PIE

3 cups whole-wheat flour
1 cup soy flour
½ cup bran

¼ cup safflower oil
1½ cups water

Mix together the dry ingredients. Run in the oil, then knead in the water until all ingredients are held together in the dough. Roll on a lightly floured board. Place bottom crust in a pie pan, cover with apple compote (recipe above), then the top crust. Bake 50 minutes in a 375° oven. Makes two crusts.

AGAR COMPOTE GELATIN

2 cups apple juice
1 stick agar

1 pint apple compote

Soak the agar in the apple juice for 10 minutes. Bring to a boil, add compote, and simmer for another 15 minutes. Pour into cups and chill. Serves four.

Vegetable Salads

CUCUMBERS IN YOGURT

1 cup plain yogurt
1 cucumber, peeled and shredded
1 teaspoon dried dill
3 cloves of garlic, finely minced

1 tablespoon vegetable oil
2 tablespoons cider vinegar
½ teaspoon vegetable salt

Mix together all ingredients except the cucumber. Pour the sauce into a bowl and mix in the cucumber. Refrigerate for two hours. Serves one.

YOGURT POTATO SALAD

1 cup plain yogurt
2 teaspoons mustard
2 teaspoons horseradish
2 cups cooked potatoes
¼ cup chopped parsley
¼ cup sliced celery

1 sliced cucumber
¼ cup sliced onion
3 cloves garlic, finely minced
1 tablespoon chopped chives
1 tablespoon chopped dill

Boil the potatoes (in their skins) until tender. Peel and chop them, and while still warm, mix them with the remaining ingredients. Refrigerate for two hours. Serves four.

SPROUT SALAD

½ lb. sprouts
¼ lb. strained sauerkraut
3 garlic cloves, finely minced
¼ lb. lettuce (or seaweed)
1 tablespoon dried dill

½ cup yogurt
1 tablespoon cider vinegar
½ tablespoon soy sauce
1 tablespoon sauerkraut juice

As the dressing, mix yogurt, vinegar, dill, soy sauce, sauerkraut juice, and garlic. Toss sprouts, sauerkraut, and lettuce in a bowl and add the dressing. Serves two. (If the salad produces flatulence, reduce the amount of sauerkraut and add ½ tablespoon carraway seeds to the recipe.)

MUSHROOM SALAD

1 lb. fresh mushrooms, sliced
½ cup vegetable oil
½ cup cider vinegar
½ cup water
2 tablespoons soy sauce

3 garlic cloves, finely minced
½ cup chopped green peppers
½ cup sliced onions
½ cup sprouts

Mix oil, vinegar, water, salt, and soy sauce, and use it to boil the garlic and onions for 3 minutes. Then simmer for 10 minutes, slowly adding the other vegetables. Refrigerate one day before serving.

Soups

BORSCH

2 cups beets
1 cup carrots
1 cup onions
1 cucumber
1 cup shredded cabbage
3 cloves garlic, finely minced

1 teaspoon vegetable salt
1 tablespoon vegetable oil
½ cup yogurt
3 teaspoons honey
4 cups water

Chop beets, carrots, onions, and garlic, and boil in two cups of water over low heat, covered, for 25 minutes. Add two more cups of water and the remaining ingredients (except yogurt) and simmer for another 10 minutes. Serve in bowls with two tablespoons of yogurt in each bowl.

GRAIN SOUP

1 small head of cabbage
1 cup whole grain (millet, rice, rye, or buckwheat)
½ cup chopped onion
½ cup celery

¼ cup parsley
3 cloves garlic, finely minced
2 tablespoons soy sauce
½ teaspoon vegetable salt
1 quart water

Cook the onion, celery, and garlic with a little water until soft. Cook the whole grain in a quart of water for 15 minutes. Add the cooked vegetables, cabbage, and seasonings to the grain and cook slowly over a low flame until the cabbage is tender. Makes five servings.

Cooked Vegetable Dishes

CABBAGE CASSEROLE

1 lb. cooked, cold cabbage	1 cup wheat germ
1 onion, chopped	1 tablespoon brewer's yeast
1 egg	2 tablespoons bran
1 teaspoon parsley, minced	½ teaspoon vegetable salt

Preheat oven to 350°. Place the cabbage, onion, egg, parsley, and garlic in a blender, and whip until smooth. Transfer to a bowl, add remaining ingredients, and mix. Place in an oiled loaf pan and bake 30 minutes. Serves five.

SPROUTS AND TOMATOES

3 cups sprouts	¼ cup chopped onion
1½ cups boiling water	2 tablespoons vegetable oil
½ teaspoon vegetable salt	1 lb. tomatoes
½ cup cabbage	1 teaspoon carraway seeds
½ cup brussels sprouts	1 teaspoon honey

Cook the bean sprouts in boiling salted water for 9 minutes, then drain. Cook the remaining vegetables (except tomatoes) in oil until tender. Add tomatoes and seasoning, and cook 5 minutes. Add the sprouts and cook a few minutes longer. Serves three.

CARROTS AND SEAWEED

1½ ounces seaweed	1 tablespoon oil
1 onion, sliced	3 tablespoons soy sauce
3 carrots, sliced	1 tablespoon wheat germ
3 gloves garlic, finely minced	1 tablespoon bran

Rinse the seaweed in cold water and soak with 2 cups of water for 15 minutes. Squeeze out the excess liquid. Sauté the onion and garlic in a little oil for a few minutes, then add the seaweed. in another few minutes, add the carrots and sauté for 5 minutes. Then pour in 1 cup of the water (used for soaking the seaweed). Bring to a boil, then let simmer over a low flame for 5 minutes. Add the wheat germ, bran, and soy sauce, and cover the pan. Simmer for another 30 minutes. Serves four.

COOKED SEAWEED

3 ounces seaweed (dulse, hiziki,
   kombu, or wakame)
3 cups cold water

2 onions, sliced
2 garlic cloves, sliced

Rinse the seaweed in a strainer with cold water. Place in a bowl and cover over with water, soaking 15 minutes. Then squeeze out the excess water (reserving the water) and cut into 1-inch pieces. Heat the oil in a pan, add the onion, garlic, and seaweed, and sauté over a high flame for 5 minutes. Pour the soaking water over the seaweed and bring to a boil. Then simmer over a low flame with partially closed lid for 30 minutes, until the water is evaporated. Serves four.

Grain Dishes

KASHA

1 teaspoon oil
1 cup buckwheat
3 cloves garlic, sliced

¼ cup bran
2¼ cups boiling water
⅛ teaspoon vegetable salt

Heat the oil in a skillet and sauté the buckwheat, bran, and garlic for a few minutes, stirring continually. Add the boiling water and salt, and cover the pan. Lower the flame and cook 15 minutes. Serves three.

KASHA CROQUETTES

2 cups cooked kasha (as above)
1 onion, minced
2 cloves garlic, minced
1 tablespoon parsley, minced

1 tablespoon soy sauce
¾ cups cooked millet
vegetable oil

Mix all ingredients except the millet and oil into a bowl. Pound the millet until it becomes like a paste. Mix with other ingredients using your fingers, wetting it frequently to prevent the dough from sticking. Shape the dough into small balls about 1 inch in diameter and sauté in oil. Serves four.

RICE CASSEROLE

1 cup rice
2 onions, sliced
3 cloves garlic, sliced
1 cup cabbage
½ cup sprouts

½ cup carrots
3 cups boiling water
4 tablespoons soy sauce
pinch of vegetable salt

Sauté the rice in a heavy saucepan. Add the boiling water and salt, and cover. Simmer 30 minutes. While the rice is cooking, sauté the vegetables. In a casserole dish, alternate layers of cooked rice with vegetables, pour soy sauce over it, and bake uncovered in a 350° oven until the top is slightly brown. Serves four.

MILLET CASSEROLE

1 cup millet
2 tablespoons bran
½ cup brussels sprouts
½ cup cabbage chunks
3 garlic cloves, sliced

1 onion, sliced
2 tablespoons vegetable oil
1 teaspoon vegetable salt
½ teaspoon dill
¼ teaspoon caraway seeds

Heat the oil in a heavy skillet, stir in the millet, bran, and onions, and brown slightly. Add the rest of the vegetables, salt, and seeds, and then stir for 3 minutes. Put the mixture into a covered saucepan, adding enough water to cover an inch over the millet. Cook over low heat for 15 minutes, then continue cooking in a double boiler until tender. Serves five.

Crackers

MARCELA'S CRACKERS

2 cups whole-wheat flour
2 cups whole-rye flour
1 cup oat flour
1½ cups rye flakes
½ cup sesame seeds
¼ cup bran
¼ cup flax seeds

⅛ cup anise seeds
⅛ cup caraway seeds
1 tablespoon salt
4 tablespoons vegetable oil
1½ cups cold water
additional ½ cup of whole-wheat
    flour to sprinkle on dough

Put all dry ingredients on a working table. With a knife, work the oil and water into them, and knead the dough with your hands. Cut off small pieces of dough about the size of Ping Pong balls and roll each ball flat until ⅛ inch thick, occasionally adding additional flour so that the dough doesn't stick. Place the slabs of dough in baking pans and bake for 20 minutes at 375°. The recipe should make 30 large crackers, which may be stored in plastic bags.

B

Practical Use of the Enema

The usual enema container holds two quarts. It is advisable to use one quart of tap water to which is added one tablespoon of epsom salts. Formulae for additional solutions and their practical applications follow.

Administering an Enema

The container is fastened two and one-half feet above the inlet. A string can be used to adjust the exact height from an object such as a door frame. Lubricate the nozzle of the tube with a vegetable oil or water-soluble K-Y jelly before inserting it into the anus. The body should be reclined on the back or the right side, with the knees brought slightly in toward the chest. The tube is pinched to control the flow, and the nozzle inserted gently into the anus. Deep and regular breathing will help the fluid enter the colon. When the amount of fluid in the colon becomes excessive, the pressure will cause discomfort. At this point, close off the tube and take out the nozzle. Before releasing the fluid and waste, it is often useful to massage the abdomen to release waste which may lie too tightly bound in the colon. To do this, lie on your back, raise both legs above body level, and rest them on a chair or against the wall. Then gently but firmly massage the whole abdominal area, moving the fingers and palms of the hands in clockwise spirals from the right side of the abdomen to the left and down. This will help the liquid flow through the obstructed areas as well as helping to disengage hardened fecal matter. Try to retain the liquid for five to fifteen minutes, and do some careful exercises, such as deep-knee bends or touching your toes. If you find this too discomforting, simply lie on your back with your knees up in the air and continue gently to massage for the duration of the time. As you progress in the technique of the enema, you will discover the amount of time most effective for you personally, and the exercises best for you. When the pressure becomes too uncomfortable, release the contents of the colon into the toilet.

Enema Formulas

1. A quart of water to which one tablespoon of salt has been added (sea salt or epsom salts). This is the formula most often recommended by both doctors and folk healers.

2. A quart of water, mixed with a tablespoon of either honey or molasses. This formula is recommended by many folk healers, and is found throughout the history of healing.

3. A quart of water, boiled with one tablespoon of fenugreek seeds, cooled and strained. This is a mild enema used in ancient India and Greece, and still used today by many naturopaths.

4. A quart of water, boiled with two tablespoons of chamomile tea, strained and cooled to warm. This formula is used in a great number of European spas. It is mild and extremely soothing.

C

CURES FOR CONSTIPATION

Russian-Ukrainian Remedies

1. Eliminate all hot drinks—tea, hot water, coffee—as well as all substances containing tannin, such as red wine and cocoa.
2. Eliminate all starchy food, particularly white bread, polished rice, potatoes, all bakery products.
3. Substitute honey for sugar.
4. Eat raw vegetables—tomatoes, lettuce, cabbage, radish, etc.—avoid sitting and passivity, and exercise early in the morning (sit-ups, etc.).
5. Every morning, massage the stomach in the direction of the colon. Start at the bottom right side of the abdomen; form small clockwise circles as you move up toward the stomach, across, and down the left side.

The Russians also offered more specific remedies in the form of preventive laxative foods:

SALT CABBAGE JUICE

1 lb. cabbage	½ lb. salt

Finely shred the raw cabbage and spread it on a wooden plank. Pour the salt over it. Wait 30 minutes until the cabbage is very moist. Squeeze the juice thoroughly. Take half a glass of this juice before every meal, and take the solid cabbage as part of your salad with the meal itself.

OAT DECOCTION

1 tablespoon oats   1 cup water

Boil the oats in a cup of water for 10 minutes. Cool, and drink at the meal.

DRIED FRUIT DECOCTION

Prepare and take like the oat decoction above.

CUCUMBER BRINE

Soak fresh cucumbers in salt water for a month. Use the brine, a full glass in the morning before breakfast.

PRUNE DECOCTION

Soak dried prunes overnight in lemon jiuce, honey, and slightly salted hot water. One glass of the infusion should be taken an hour before breakfast and the prunes eaten for breakfast, with sour milk, yogurt, or buttermilk.

East European Remedies

1. East-Europeans take sauerkraut and sauerkraut juice to relieve constipation. The juice is taken before the meals, and the solid portion eaten alone as part of the meal, or placed in a salad with other vegetables. The high fiber content provides the bulk needed for peristalsis, while the alkaline content reduces acidity associated with digestive disorder, and the lactic acid aids the friendly bacteria of the colon that aid in digestion.

2. The lactic acid is also gained by eating large quantities of other soured products such as sour cucumbers or pickles, and soured-milk products such as yogurt, kefir, buttermilk, cottage cheese, and whey.

3. People in all parts of the world, throughout the history of folk medicine, have found relief from constipation by eating garlic. It can be eaten raw, by itself, if one is especially courageous, but mixed with milk or yogurt it is more palatable, and with leafy green vegetables it is less offensive to others within range of the odor. The allicin in the garlic passes into the intestine and stimulates peristaltic motion of the bowels, promoting more effective bowel movement.

D

Exercises to Alleviate Constipation and Aid Elimination

The Hunza "Stomach Lift"

Stand erect, keeping your feet apart. Inhale deeply, exhale, and without taking a new breath, pull your abdomen in so that it becomes hollow. Now bend the knees forward slightly, place hands on thighs, inclining the body a little forward. Do not breathe at all while in action. Now pull the stomach in and out, repeating it as long as you can hold your breath without feeling tired. Return to the original posture and repeat the exercise ten times. This posture strengthens abdominal muscles and helps to reduce constipation and indigestion.

Oriental Two-step Remedy for Constipation

1. Stand firm on the floor. Place hands on hips. Gently lower yourself into a squatting position. Repeat up to 25 times.
2. Lie down. Massage your stomach with your arm, which should be wrapped in a towel. Massage from your ribcage down to your pelvic bones in all directions. Use very little

pressure. Repeat this for up to 15 minutes. It is reported that these exercises help loosen intestinal-digestive congestion and promote natural regularity.

American Deep-knee Bends and Other Exercises

1. Begin with five or six bends at a time, working up gradually until squatting at least 20 times a day.
2. Lying flat on a mat on the floor and exercising the legs with the bicycle movement is also good.
3. Throw the arms around the thighs and rock back and forth on the curved back.
4. Stand up and pretend to pull the abdominal wall upward and backward under the ribs, and then relax. After getting used to it, repeat about 20 times.

In each case, it is advised that if you are not used to exercises, it is best to begin with a few and gradually increase to the right number. This avoids extreme soreness from overusing unused muscles.

E

Laxative Recipes and Formulas

Laxative Food Recipes

AN ANCIENT BYELORUSSIAN METHOD

1 fresh unpeeled cucumber
3 tablespoons honey

juice of three lemons

Thinly slice the cucumbers, and place in a deep plate. Then mix the honey and lemon juice, and pour it over the cucumbers. Leave about an hour. This is to be eaten with each of the three meals.

BREAKFAST LAXATIVE MEAL #1 (BARLEY MIXTURE)

¼ cup pearled barley
2 quarts water
2 raw figs

½ teaspoon cut licorice root
2 tablespoons raisins

Boil the barley in water. When the water has boiled down to about one quart, strain carefully. Slice the figs and add with other ingredients, mix, and boil for 5 minutes. Strain. First eat the solid portion, then slowly sip the liquid portion.

BREAKFAST LAXATIVE MEAL #2

¼ cup wheat bran
¼ cup whole linseed
1 tablespoon ground barley
4 figs, cut up

3 prunes, pitted
2 tablespoons raisins
½ cup buttermilk or yogurt

161

Boil the grains and dried fruit in water for 5 minutes, then add the honey and buttermilk or (yogurt), and eat as breakfast.

BREAKFAST LAXATIVE MEAL #3

¼ cup flaxseed	1 cup water
¼ cup bran	1 tablespoon raisins
1 apple, cut up	1 tablespoon vegetable oil

Boil the grains and the apple for 5 minutes in the water. Then add the remaining ingredients and serve.

OAT TONIC (BEFORE-BREAKFAST DRINK)

2 tablespoons oats   1 glass water

Boil the oats in water for 5 minutes. Cool and eat before breakfast.

PRUNE TONIC (BEFORE-BREAKFAST DRINK)

1 cup dried prunes	2 tablespoons honey
juice of three lemons	2 cups water

Boil the water and pour it over the other ingredients in a glass jar. Leave overnight at room temperature. The next morning, drink one glass of the liquid per hour, twice before breakfast. Eat the solid portion as part of breakfast.

FIG TONIC (BEFORE-BREAKFAST DRINK)

2 tablespoons vegetable oil (preferably linseed oil)	1 cup dried figs

Soak the figs in oil overnight and eat them first thing in morning.

LEMON TONIC (BEFORE-BREAKFAST DRINK)

1 cup warm water   juice of two lemons

Squeeze the lemons into the warm water and drink upon arising in morning.

CABBAGE TONIC (BEFORE-BREAKFAST DRINK)

2 cups pressed cabbage juice

Drink every morning before breakfast.

CUCUMBER TONIC (BEFORE-BREAKFAST DRINK)

1 finely cut cucumber   ½ cup salt water or kelp-in-water

Soak the cucumbers in salt water for several hours and drink the water in the morning before breakfast.

TIBETAN VEGETABLE JUICE TONIC
(BEFORE ANY MEALS)

1 quart vegetable juice   1 finely cut onion
(preferably liquefied, but
may be juice from boiled
vegetables)

Fill a glass bottle with juice, add the cut onion, and let it remain in a warm place overnight. Strain. Use just 2 teaspoons of this tonic twice daily before meals, in a glass of cold water.

Laxative foods

Raw Honey. Eating several tablespoons of raw honey as a tonic every day seems to have a lubricating effect on the intestinal tract.

Agar-agar helps to form a smooth slippery bulk in the intestinal tract and acts as a natural regulator of the bowels. It can be boiled into a jelly and used as a base for soups and puddings.

Garlic has been known for centuries as an antibacterial agent, an extremely effective regulator of blood pressure, and an aid to peristalsis. It can be eaten raw, several times daily with green leafy vegetables to mitigate the offensive odor.

Yogurt, kefir, buttermilk, and *soured milk* have been used for thousands of years by Europeans and Asians as a highly nutritious source of calcium and protein, as well as a digestive aid and regulator of the bowels.

Sauerkraut, sour pickles, and *sour rye bread* also have a stimulating effect on the friendly bacteria of the intestinal tract which establish regularity of bowel function.

F

Home Treatment of Diarrhea

We have compiled a list of home remedies for diarrhea that might be used as directed. In the first section we include those recipes most often used and prescribed by medical practitioners. In the second section we include several remedies used by folk healers, and in the third section we list the herbs most commonly used by folk healers throughout the ages. All of these remedies have one thing in common—they are primarily warmed water, which is exactly what is required during a diarrhea bout. The herbs used are in such small quantity as to be of absolutely no danger to the system. Moreover, if hundreds, perhaps thousands of years of careful use have selected out these herbs as of value in this condition, there is every reason to believe that they may do some good.

Prescribed Medical Treatments

THE TWO-GLASS METHOD

GLASS NO. 1

8 ounces orange, apple, or other fruit juice (rich in potassium)

½ teaspoon honey or corn syrup or molasses (rich in glucose necessary for absorption of essential salts)

pinch of table salt (sodium chloride)

GLASS NO. 2

8 ounces tap water (boiled or carbonated)	¼ teaspoon baking soda (sodium bicarbonate)

Drink alternately from each glass.

BURMA FRUIT CORDIAL

5 grams table salt	juice of ½ lime
2 pints water	

BOUILLION

1 cup boiling water	½ teaspoon vegetable or meat extract
¼ teaspoon honey or molasses	

Each of the three treatments requires sipping these drinks throughout the day at intervals, up to three to four glasses per day.

Folk Remedies

Dysentery Cure

This remedy was used by Russian soldiers at the front during World War I. The patient took a tablespoon of warm water saturated with salt and refrained from all food and drink for 24 hours. (We have already learned of the body's need for salt during diarrhea, and as we have shown in Chapter 6, fasting would certainly be of value.)

Apple Therapy

First a cleansing enema with a chamomile infusion was taken, and a complete fast for 24 hours. Then for the next 24 hours the patient was given two medium apples, peeled, cored, and grated—every 4 hours. No other food or drink was given. Cures were completed within the 24 hours. (The enema and the fast seem good advice. The pectin content of the apples provides a soft absorptive mass which releases and carries out bacteria from the colon walls.)

Black Bread Ash

Burned black bread was reduced to ash, ground, and taken as follows: one teaspoonful of ash in a small wineglass of red wine once a day, and repeated on the second day if necessary. (The ash would offer us the carminative relief found in over-the-counter charcoal remedies, the wine offers us a bit of potassium and sucrose and some astringency, and then, of course, there is the liquid content.)

Traditional Herbal Cures

The following herbs have been found by folk healers, from ancient times until today, to have been effective against *extended* diarrhea. We must add that a day or so of diarrhea was not considered very serious and that herbal cures may not even have been introduced until the second or third day of diarrhea.

Amaranth *(Amaranthus hypochondriacus)*

In folklore, this flower is regarded as the symbol of immortality. The name is taken from the Greek word *amarantos,* meaning "incorruptible." The ancient Greeks spread amaranth flowers over the graves of the dead to show their belief in the immortality of the soul. Homer wrote that the people of Thessaly wore crowns of amaranth at the burial of Achilles.

Containing a large amount of vitamins and minerals, amaranth was used in place of spinach in the Middle Ages. Throughout history, it was used as an astringent in the treatment of diarrhea and dysentery. The herb is dried, powdered, and half a teaspoon put into a pint of boiling water. The pint is sipped four or five times a day until the condition clears up.

Cloves *(Eugenia caryophyllata)*

Cloves were introduced to Venice by the Arabs and from there distributed to the rest of Europe. Cloves are flower buds that come from a tree now grown in such places as Zanzibar and the Moluccas.

Most of our readers know of its use as oil of cloves for traditional relief of toothaches. However, it has also been widely used for relief of diarrhea and dysentery. Add ¼ teaspoon of the powder to a cup of boiling water and sip it. It can be mixed with other herbs as a soothing mechanism.

Garlic

The Chinese, Greeks, Romans, Hindus, Egyptians, and Babylonians all claimed that garlic cured intestinal disorders such as diarrhea and dysentery. Today, it is used throughout Russia and East European countries to such an extent that it is called Russian penicillin. Experiments completed in East Europe show that garlic decreases the amount of putrefactive bacteria while increasing the number of "friendly bacteria." Garlic, taken like raw cloves as powder or as capsules, has proved enormously effective in cases of *chronic* diarrhea.

Myrrh *(Balsamodendron myrrha)*

Myrrh is a tree native to lands bordering the Red Sea. The bark gives off a juice which hardens into drops of gum. The ancient Egyptians used myrrh in the embalming of their mummies and the ancient Hebrews used it as a holy oil in the anointing of the Tabernacle and Ark as well as a drug for the purification of women. Additionally, it has been used throughout history as a cure for chronic diarrhea. A teaspoon of myrrh in a pint of boiling water, taken three times a day, is said to cure the most stubborn cases in less than a week. It may also be mixed effectively with golden seal powder (Hydrastis), equal parts of each, in boiling water.

Peppermint *(Mentha piperita)*

Various kinds of mint have been popular since ancient times and were mentioned in the New Testament as "thithes of mint." It has traditionally been used for weakness of the stomach, most effectively in cases of sudden diarrhea. Essence of peppermint is most often cited in historical sources, but a brew of the dried leaves is also effective. As soon as the attack of diarrhea comes on, drop 15 drops of essence into a cup of boiling water and sip. Repeat every three hours. Instead of 15 drops of essence, a teaspoon of the dried herb may be used.

Slippery Elm *(Ulmus fulva)*

The inner bark of the slippery elm was used extensively by American Indians and early settlers as a demulcent, to absorb noxious gases and to neutralize stomach acidity. Because of its mucilaginous nature, it gently passes through the intestinal system where other foods would be rejected. An ounce of the powdered bark is mixed in a pint of boiling water, forming a mucilage, which is taken three times a day until the diarrhea is cured.

Papaya

We have extolled the digestive benefits of papaya in Chapter 3. It is important to mention here that the fresh fruit of the papaya has been used by natives of the tropics for hundreds of years for relief from diarrhea.

CARMINATIVE TONICS

To improve digestion through elimination of excessive gas, try the following:

2 parts spearmint leaves
2 parts valerian root

1 part chamomile flowers

Mix 2 teaspoons in a cup of boiling water. Infuse, strain, sip.

1 part chamomile flowers

1 part majoram

Mix 1 tablespoon in a cup of boiling water. Infuse, strain, sip.

1 part chamomile flowers
1 part spearmint leaves

1 part caraway seeds

Mix 2 teaspoons in a cup of boiling water. Infuse, strain, sip.

3 parts chamomile flowers   or
3 parts fennel seeds
2 parts valerian root

3 parts fennel seed
2 parts caraway seed
1 part majoram

Mix 1 teaspoon in a cup of boiling water. Infuse, strain, sip.

A mixture of ⅓ teaspoon of golden seal root (powdered) in a cup of boiling water, taken within an hour before meals, helps to stimulate digestion and prevent large gas buildup during the meal.

Index